Rescue Me
A Guide to Pet Rҽ

Jade

Author: Paul E. Love

Copyright 2011 Paul E. Love

Contact Information
  Email address: ioxbooks@gmail.com

  ioxbooks (ioxcom)

Other titles by ioxbooks:
   The Employer's Payroll Question and Answer Book
   Web Apps the Easy Way with ASP.NET Maker
   The Pet Menagerie
   The UAV Question and Answer Book

"Rescue Me" - Aretha Franklin

Rescue me
Oh take me in your arms
Rescue me
I want your tender charms
'Coz I'm lonely and I'm blue
I need you and your love too

... the hardest part is the dogs who have had a home and every time people come around they run to the front of the cage looking for their people to come back and get them – then they slowly give up hope and don't even look up anymore when someone walks by ...

CONTENTS

Introduction

Each year somewhere around 6 to 8 million dogs, cats and other animals in the United States end up in shelters - and about half of those are eventually euthanized. The number of these "animals in need" has reached epidemic proportions and continues to grow. "No kill" and "low kill" shelters are forced to turn away animals because they simply don't have room for them.

In spite of tireless efforts to find homes for everyone, the flood of lost, abandoned, and simply unwanted animals pushes shelters and rescue groups to the limit. Owners who don't bother to spay or neuter their pets, puppy mills, animals turned in because of "bad behavior", people who give up a pet because it turned out to different that they thought it would be, senior citizens forced to give up their pets due to financial or health problems - there are a variety of reasons for the influx of homeless animals but the result is huge numbers of dogs, cats and others that will never find a "forever home".

Over the years my wife and I, along with our two daughters and my mother-in-law, have brought a variety of dogs, cats and birds into our home and most of them have been rescues. Why do we do it? I suppose it's because it's so hard to turn your back on anything that is in desperate need and can't help itself. And, not to be trite, but they have given back so much in return and have asked very little.

I guess we could be considered to have "done our part" by adopting these animals, but in spite of that (or maybe because of it) we also volunteer at a local shelter. I think the main reason we volunteered is that we see all of the dogs and cats we've given a home to reflected in those that are living in cages, waiting for someone to come along and give them a home. They don't ask for much, just a chance to have a family, people to love and a place where they belong and someone cares about them – pretty much what any of us want out of life.

I know that we all have plenty of other things to deal with besides animals in shelters. But if you or anyone you know is thinking about getting a dog, cat or other animal, please contact your local "city pound", animal shelter, or special breed rescue group and take a look at some of these homeless animals. If you're looking for a great companion, there are so many of them there - confused, scared and in many cases on what amounts to "death row" - please consider giving one of them a second chance.

NOTE: Throughout this book the male pronoun is used at times to refer to dogs and cats in general; no chauvinism is intended – it's simply done to avoid calling a living thing "it" or having to continually write "he or she" or "him or her". (Besides which, with our parrots, short of a DNA test or one of them laying an egg, there's really no way to tell him from her so either pronoun may apply).

Animals In Need

Q: Why are there so many animals in need?
A: Every year shelters and rescue groups take in around 6 to 8 million dogs, cats and other animals – and about half of them end up being euthanized. It's simply not possible to place that many animals. There are a lot of reasons why there are so many homeless animals: lack of spaying and neutering, lost pets, animals left behind when their owners move, older people who can't afford to take care of their pets anymore, and animals turned loose simply because they turned out to be bigger, or more energetic, or just more trouble than their owners thought they would be.

Q: How many people get pets from shelters compared to breeders or pet stores?
A: One study indicates that less than 20 percent of the approximately 59 million pets in the United States are shelter adoptees. Why are so few taken from shelters? Part of the answer is that people have a number of misconceptions about the dogs and cats available at shelters, such as:
- Most shelter pets are older
- The majority of animals at shelters are sick or have major behavior problems
- You can't get purebred animals at a shelter
- Visiting a shelter is depressing

Q: What if I want a specific breed of dog or cat?
A: About 25 percent of all shelter animals are purebred dogs and cats. And if your shelter doesn't

have what you want, there's probably a local rescue group for the particular breed you're trying to find.

Q: Aren't most shelter animals older? I want a young animal.
A: Actually the majority of dogs and cats in shelters are usually from 1 to 2 years old.

Q: I really don't want to go to a shelter - aren't most shelters really depressing places?
A: They can be – some "city pounds" are a whole lot like prisons, with concrete block rooms packed with cages and a multitude of dogs or cats. However many shelters have clean, well-lighted, roomy kennels or cat rooms, and even "get acquainted" areas where you can spend some one-on-one time with a dog or cat you're interested in adopting. Also, a lot of shelters and rescue groups hold "adoption events" at various locations such as stores or parks, where you can come and meet some of the dogs and cats that are available for adoption without going to the actual shelter.

Q: Do shelters only take in dogs and cats?
A: The great majority of the animals at most shelters are dogs and cats, but they may also take in other animals such as horses, rabbits, birds, hamsters, guinea pigs, ferrets and reptiles.

Q: My shelter charges from $100 to $150 to adopt a dog or cat – isn't that too much?
A: Not really. Shelters need to recover the cost of housing, feeding, spaying or neutering, vaccinations and possibly even basic obedience training. Another reason for charging a fairly high adoption fee may be

to make sure the person doing the adopting is serious about taking care of the animal and is ready to handle the financial burden of taking on a pet. Most shelters will take back a pet that was adopted from the shelter, but the object is to make sure the new owner fully understands the responsibilities and expenses involved so adopted pets aren't brought back. Also, if you buy from a breeder or pet store you will probably be paying $200 to $300 or more and possibly encouraging a puppy mill operation.

Note: If the adoption charges are very high – say $300 or more, be cautious. Some puppy mills and other for-profit organizations operate under the guise of a shelter or rescue group.

Q: What exactly is a "puppy mill"?
A: Puppy mills are large commercial "for profit" operations that are only concerned with how much money they can make. Dogs used for breeding are often kept caged in poor conditions for as long as they remain fertile – when they are no longer useful the breeding animals are often killed, abandoned or sold for scientific research. The result of these type of operations is millions of puppies, many with behavior or health problems. Also, puppy mill dogs are often sold as purebred dogs in order to get a higher price for them when in fact (because of indiscriminate breeding practices) many of them are actually mixed breeds.

Q: The shelter wants me to fill out a lengthy application – why?
A: Normally shelters want to make sure that a pet doesn't end up in the wrong hands – an irresponsible

9

owner, someone looking for a dog to train for dog fighting, and so on. It's usually easy enough to get approved and a little extra time filling out paperwork shouldn't matter that much when you're adopting a new member of the family that could be with you for the next 10 to 15 years. However don't be afraid to ask what the adoption fee includes, what's expected of you when you sign the contract, and what the shelter or other group will do to assist you. Also ask what happens if for some reason you cannot keep the animal; most organizations ask that you return the dog or cat to them if you can no longer care for it.

Q: I just saw the questionnaire the shelter wants me to fill out – what right do they have to ask some of these questions?
A: Shelter adoption questionnaires may include questions like:
- Are you planning to move in the next six months?
- What is the average noise/activity level in your home?
- How often do you plan to vaccinate this pet?
- What percentage of the time will this pet spend outside?
- If you find you can no longer take care of the pet what will you do?
- Do you have a regular veterinarian?
- If you have other pets are they currently licensed and/or carry ID tags or other identification?

- Please list all pets you have had in the last 10 years, whether the pet still lives with you and if not, what happened to him or her?

And a number of other "personal" questions. The reason for these type of questions is simply to try to make sure the person is going to provide a stable, safe and healthy home for the animal and to provide a "checklist" of sorts of things to consider when adopting a rescue animal.

Q: Should older people adopt a shelter dog or cat?

A: Studies have shown that having a pet around can help relieve stress and anxiety and lower the risk of heart attack or stroke, particularly among older people. Pets also give their owners the feeling of being needed, an important factor in keeping older owners involved in everyday living. Of course for most people in their later years adopting an adult dog or cat and one that has a more laid-back disposition usually works out best.

Q: Is it better to adopt a purebred or a mixed breed dog?

A: There isn't any "right" answer when it comes to purebred versus mixed breed. However, there are a couple things to keep in mind: purebreds are usually scarce at a shelter – your best bet is often a rescue group that specializes in a particular breed. Also purebreds tend to be more susceptible to certain genetic problems such as allergies or hip dysplasia.

On the other hand you have a pretty good idea of what type of dog you're getting if you adopt a border collie, a chihuahua, or a dalmatian; mixed breeds are just that – a mix of different characteristics.

Q: What is "big black dog syndrome"?

A: Big black dog syndrome is a phenomenon where big black dogs (and black cats) in shelters or rescue groups tend to be passed over or ignored entirely by potential adopters. People seem to have a natural bias toward lighter-colored animals; when asked why the explanations range from "black animals tend to be mean" to "you can't see the expression on the face of a black animal". The most generally accepted theory is that people associate the color black with evil or misfortune and that affects their choice of a dog or cat. Because of this "BBD" or "Big Black Dog" syndrome, shelters often make a special effort to make their black dogs and cats more appealing.

Author's note: My very big and very black Labradane strongly disagrees with the idea that big black dogs should be avoided – however he does feel that big black dogs don't get nearly enough cheeseburgers.

Q: I want a young dog to train as a guard dog – can I find one at a shelter?

A: At most shelters you can find many different dogs that are trainable as guard dogs. However, unless you have a great deal of experience with guard dogs, it's best to get a professional to train your dog. And while you're at it, get some training yourself so you're comfortable handling the dog and know how to handle him in different situations.

Q: What is "fostering"?
A: Foster "parents" provide a temporary home for animals in need. "Temporary" may mean anything from a few days to several months depending on the amount of care required or how much behavioral work needs to be done. Fostering is done for a variety of reasons: limited shelter space, very young animals that require special care, or animals that are ill or injured and need additional help.

Animals being fostered should be introduced slowly and carefully to children or other pets to determine compatibility – and in the case of animals who have undergone emotional or physical trauma, to give the animal being fostered a chance to adjust to its new environment.

In some case the fostering family may decide to keep the dog, cat or other animal but whether they do or not, fostering can give a homeless animal a real chance at being adopted and finding a permanent home.

Author's note: We recently took two kittens from a local animal shelter the day before they were scheduled to be euthanized. We dewormed the kittens, kept them separated from our other pets unless we were there to supervise things, and managed to find homes for both of them after about three weeks (although it seemed longer – kittens have an amazing amount of energy). It's always a little hectic trying to fit "outsiders" into your normal household routine but fostering can definitely be worth the effort.

Author's note #2: One caution about fostering. A few years ago we took in a cockatoo that had been badly traumatized. We intended to get it healthy again so a friend of ours could adopt it. When our friend came to get "Gabriel", Gabby was panicked and alternated between huddling in a corner and trying frantically to get to my daughter. Needless to say Gabriel is still with us. If the animal you're fostering is badly damaged emotionally and forms a very strong bond with its foster parent or parents it may be a real problem giving it up.

Q: I just adopted a dog from the shelter and he seems restless, hardly eats any of his food and seems really jumpy – what's up?
A: Remember that your new dog is trying to adjust to his new home – he wants to please you but he's not sure yet what you expect of him. Plus he doesn't know if he's going to be staying or if you're going to take him and leave him somewhere else. Be patient and he should settle down after a few days when he begins to feel more comfortable and secure.

Q: I've got a behavior problem with the pet I just adopted – who can I ask for advice?
A: A worker at the shelter may be able to help or you can ask your veterinarian. You can also go online at www.aspcabehavior.org , type in your pet's behavior problem and you can step-by-step advice from ASPCA experts 24 hours a day.

Q: How do I recognize animal abuse and who do I report it to?

A: There are certain signs and symptoms that are common in most cases of animal cruelty:

- Limping
- Patches of missing hair
- Wounds on the body
- Extremely thin animals with the ribcage and backbone showing
- Animals kept outside in extreme weather or left chained outside without food or water
- Animals that cower in fear or bark and snarl at the approach of their owner
- Seeing an owner actually physically abusing an animal

Your first step in reporting an instance of animal cruelty is normally to contact the police and give them all the details you can. If the police can't help you can try the animal control department or the local humane organization.

Rescuing Stray Animals

Q: What sort of things should I keep around the house or in my car for rescuing a stray cat or dog?
A: Here's a short list of items you may need if you are trying to rescue a stray:
  • Carrier or crate
  • Blanket
  • Collapsible water bowl and bottled water
  • Collar and leash
  • Strong-smelling food such as canned tuna
  • First-aid kit for pets
  • Phone numbers for your local animal control agency, shelter and 24-hour veterinary hospital

Q: What if I see a stray dog or cat in the street or about to go out into the street?
A: If you can do so safely, turn on your emergency blinkers and pull completely off the road. When you get out of your car, don't make any sudden moves that could spook the dog or cat. If he's in the street try to coax him back off the road. Approach him carefully, speak calmly and, if you have some strong-smelling food with you, use that to try to get him to come to you. If the stray is a dog and it starts to growl, raise his hackles, or bear his teeth, back off and call for help.

If you know someone who can come immediately to get the animal, you can try to lure him into your car (it's not a good idea to try to drive anywhere with an unrestrained dog or cat). If you don't know someone to call, you can try contacting the local animal control agency or the police or sheriff. And if you're worried about what will happen once the dog or cat is taken to a shelter, follow it to the shelter and get his animal control number – then if no owner is found you have the option to step in and adopt or foster the animal.

If you can't contact anyone and you're sure you can transport the animal safely you can take him to a shelter or a veterinarian. If you decide to take the dog or cat home with you, check for a collar and ID tag – if there isn't any ID tag, take him to a shelter or veterinarian as soon as possible so they can check to see if he's been microchipped.

Also, if you take the animal home keep him separate from any of your own pets. It's possible that he's sick or may be aggressive toward other animals.

Q: What if I rescue a dog or cat that's injured?
A: If you take an injured animal to a veterinarian be prepared to take financial responsibility before treatment begins. If you're committed to trying to save an injured animal discuss possible courses of treatment and what charges are involved. Your other option is to take the injured dog or cat to your local animal control agency or shelter; they may or may not be able to accept the animal and may or may not have the facilities to treat him. Also, some shelters will take the dog or cat and care for it without charge, while others may want you to pay for any treatment.

Q: Can you get sick from handling a stray cat?
A: It is possible to catch cat scratch disease (CSD), also known as "cat scratch fever" if you're bitten or scratched by an infected cat. Cat scratch fever is a bacterial infection and the bacteria can live on in the lymph nodes for some time after the bite or scratch heals. Symptoms include:

- Mild fever
- Headache
- Flu-like symptoms
- Swelling near the scratch or bite
- Swollen lymph nodes

Effects of cat scratch fever normally clear up within 2 to 4 weeks. However in a few cases CSD can persist, with more serious results: sores all over the body, damage to the spleen, and even swelling of the brain. The bottom line: if you're scratched or bitten by a stray cat have your doctor check it out.

Q: If I've found a stray what should I do to try to find the owners?
A: Assuming the animal doesn't have ID tags or a microchip, put up posters with a general description of the cat or dog (and a picture if possible) and include your phone number(s). Be sure to withhold some information about the dog or cat and ask anyone who calls to claim him to supply that information. You can also check with your local shelter to see if the animal may be on their "lost animal" list. Most newspapers provide free ads in the classified section for found dogs and you can also post information on websites such as petfinder.org and craigslist.com for free.

Q: What if I want to keep a stray (or give him to someone else) and have him spayed or neutered?

A: Most places have regulations about how long a dog or cat is considered a stray. You can't legally spay or neuter or re-home a stray animal until that waiting period is over.

Helping Your Local Shelter

Q: What's the most important thing I can do to help a shelter or rescue group?
A: The single most important thing anyone can do is to spay and neuter your pets and to encourage every pet owner you know to do the same with their pets. Finding shelter animals new homes isn't the real answer to dealing with the millions of animals in shelters – spaying and neutering pets will help stop the flood of animals at its source.

Q: I want to help my local animal shelter – can I donate something besides money?
A: Animal shelters and rescue groups are always in need of a variety of items. In addition to monetary donations shelters usually welcome things such as:
- Quilts, sheets, old towels and blankets or any other type of bedding
- Durable leashes and collars (all sizes)
- No-spill food bowls
- Rawhide chews
- Canned or dry dog and cat food (name brands)
- Kitty litter (non-clumping) and litter pans
- Dog and cat toys (kongs, nylabones, heavy rope toys, etc.)
- Dog sweaters (all sizes)
- Medical supplies (syringes, clean-up wipes, rubber gloves)
- Cleaning products (paper towels, baby wipes, brooms, Lysol, storage bags, etc.)
- Dog crates and cat carriers
- Fans

- Puppy pads, pet baby bottles, dry baby cereal, distilled water, X-pens
- Flea and tick control products
- Office supplies – postage stamps, ink pens, batteries, file folders, markers, Post-It notes
- Gift certificates to pet stores or office supply stores

Q: What about fund raising?
A: There are a multitude of ways to go about raising funds for a shelter or rescue group:
- Have a yard sale and donate the money to a shelter
- Put together a pet treat cookbook and donate the money from sales of the cookbook
- Put together a bake sale
- Have a candy fundraiser
- Sponsor a sports tournament with ticket proceeds and entry fees going to a shelter
- Have a dog wash or car wash
- Create a pet calendar with sales going to the shelter
- Host a bingo night and donate admission proceeds
- Make costumes or other decorations for special holiday adoption events
- Charge admission to a costume contest for dogs and cats
- Ask a local pet supply store to donate a small percentage of their sales on a certain holiday or weekend
- Have a raffle

Q: What about volunteering?
A: Shelters and rescue groups are almost always in need of additional (unpaid) help. If you are really interested in helping out at the shelter or at adoption events, contact the shelter or rescue group and get some information on whether they need volunteers and if so, what kind of work you might be doing.

Volunteer work at a shelter usually involves things like:
- Feeding, exercising and socializing dogs and cats
- Cleaning kennels or other areas
- Washing bedding and toys
- Assisting with obedience training
- Taking photos or videos of animals available for adoption
- Helping to repair or build animal pens or other structures
- Assisting with office work
- Transporting animals or equipment to and from adoption events
- Assisting at adoption events by showing animals, setting up, cleaning up, etc.

Author's note: Getting to know some of the dogs and cats at a shelter and watching them go unadopted and, in some cases, end up being euthanized can be a little hard on you emotionally at times. There are the highs of seeing your favorites find new "forever" homes and the lows of seeing really great pets that no one seems to want – and some pets that just seem to give up and withdraw into themselves. It's a great way to help those who can't help themselves, but you have to make sure you don't get so involved that you "burn out".

Q: How can I find out where to volunteer?
A: You can go to www.volunteermatch.org to find places to volunteer based on your location and the type of work you would like to do.

Q: Are there any other ways to help?
A: There are a number of other ways to help:
- Start a drive in your neighborhood or town to get pet owners to make sure their pets have ID tags or some other form of identification. Out of all the lost pets brought to shelters, only 16% of the dogs and 2% of the cats are ever reunited with their owners. Those percentages could increase significantly if owners would simply make sure their pets carry some form of identification.
- Encourage anyone you know that is looking for a pet to adopt from a shelter or rescue group and to avoid buying from pet stores (unless the store's animals come from a shelter).
- Pick up stray animals and try to help find their owners; go door-to-door, post flyers and put an ad in the paper. If all that fails, then take the animal to a shelter and give them as much information as possible about the animal – where and when you found it, what condition it was in, and so forth.
- "Friend" your local rescues on Facebook and re-post their notices about fundraisers or adoption events.

- If your shelter or rescue group has a "wish list" on their web site of items they would like people to donate, post a link to that list on your Facebook page. Many people don't realize that shelters can make use of a lot of the items they have lying around the house and don't need anymore.
- The Animal Rescue Site runs several contests per year that award money to local shelters. By visiting the website and voting once per day you can help your favorite shelter or rescue group win a cash prize grant. Sixty-nine grants totaling $75,000 will be awarded this year (2011). Just go to: http://www.theanimalrescuesite.com, click on the "Shelter Challenge" tab. When the new page displays, type in the name of the shelter you want to vote for, select the state where it is located and hit "Search". Once the name and address of your shelter displays confirm your vote by typing in the verification code.
- Freekibble.com and Feekibblekat.com donate ten pieces of kibble to shelter pets when you answer a daily trivia question at one or both of their sites.
- If you're planning to send flowers order through www.teleflora.com/aspca and 20% of your purchase price will be donated to the ASPCA.
- Do your web surfing using www.goodsearch.com. GoodSearch is a Yahoo-powered search engine that donates 50% of its revenues to charitable causes and

users can choose which cause their searches benefit.

- Shop online using www.goodshop.com. GoodShop is an online shopping mall launched by GoodSearch. It's affiliated with over a thousand retailers (including Amazon, eBay, Target, Best Buy, and Staples) and a percentage of each purchase goes to your designated charity.
- By doing a web search for "support animal rescue" you can come up with sites like "Cork for a Cause" (http://www.corkforacause.com) that run special programs from time to time to help various causes. Currently, as this is being written, "Corks for a Cause" is providing 112 bowls of food to rescued animals for every "Animal Rescue" bottle of wine purchased on their website. An hour or so spent searching will normally turn up a few other sites running similar promotions.

Q: What about offering professional services?
A: Animal shelters often have need for professionals who can help with things like website design, accounting, or photography. In fact one very successful partnership involves photographers who have donated their services to local shelters to provide photos of dogs, cats and other animals using professional lighting and props – and adoptions at those shelters have increased as much as 100 percent.

Making Shelter Animals More Adoptable

Q: What are some ways for shelter workers and volunteers to make dogs more adoptable?

A: There are a number of things that can be done to make a dog more adoptable:

- Make sure the dog is well groomed and well fed
- Socialize the dog to ensure that it's well behaved around strangers and other dogs (and cats if possible)
- Perform some basic obedience training so the dog will obey simple commands such as "sit", "heel", "off", "leave it", and "stay".
- Some shelters are beginning to offer agility training – that can also be a plus for people interested in canine agility competitions
- Make sure the dog has had all necessary vaccinations and has been spayed or neutered
- Provide a pleasant, homey looking area where people can look at and meet animals they may be interested in adopting

Q: What does basic obedience training involve?

A: Beginning obedience training courses usually last from about 6 to 10 weeks – long enough for the dog to learn the commands and (hopefully) respond to them consistently. As a rule the dog is trained on one command at a time, usually beginning with learning to walk under control on a leash.

The basic commands are:

- Sit

- Down (the dog's elbows and rear legs should be touching the ground)
- Heel (the dog is walking beside you on your left side with his head even with your leg)
- Come or Here (calls the dog to you)
- Stay (the dog must remain in his current position until you release him)
- Stand (the dog stands still – if in a sit or down position the dog stands up)

Some additional commands:
- Stop (tells the dog to stop whatever he's doing and stay where he is)
- Back Up
- Steady (stay near by)
- Off (if the dog is jumping up on something, this command tells the dog to stop and get down)
- Drop It (tells the dog to drop whatever it has hold of)
- Leave It (tells the dog not to touch an item)
- Take It (tells the dog to pick up a certain item)
- Give (the dog "hands over" whatever item he has in his mouth)

And of course there are a few more that you can work on such as "roll over", "shake", "high 5", "play dead", and so on.

Author's Note: I have heard of obedience training for cats (using a clicker and plenty of treats) but have yet to see it done in person. It's certainly not necessary to train a cat to come eat (they can hear the sound of a refrigerator door opening from the other side of the house). As for basic obedience commands, my experience is that a cat will sit and stare at you for a few minutes as you try to teach them a command then they get bored with silly human antics and wander off to take a nap.

Q: What is "agility training"?
A: Fashioned after horse jumping, Agility has become the fastest growing dog sport. Handlers direct their dog through an obstacle course while being judged for time and accuracy. The handler can't touch either the dog or the obstacles; he or she has to control the dog with voice and body signals.

Agility courses consist of a set of obstacles laid out by a judge in an area with a surface of grass, dirt or rubber. In most cases the obstacles are marked with a number or have a numbered cone next to them indicating the order in which they have to be completed.

Typical obstacles include weave poles, a tunnel, a dog walk, winged jumps, a teeter-totter, tire jumps, a pause table, an A-frame, and a collapsed tunnel or "chute".

A few shelters offer programs that let volunteer handlers train certain dogs to negotiate agility courses. The training helps keep the dogs in top physical condition and gives them something to look forward to – and it can be a real plus for potential adopters who want a dog they can compete with on agility courses.

Adopting a Pet Can Benefit Your Health

Q: How can a dog or cat improve your health?
A: Here are a few of the health benefits of owning a pet:

- According to the Centers for Disease Control (CDC) pets can lower your blood pressure, especially in people with hypertension. Just petting an animal can cause a person's blood pressure to drop. A study by researchers at the State University of New York measured the effect of pet ownership on 48 stockbrokers being treated for hypertension and found that the 24 brokers who had a pet had significantly more of a reduction in high blood pressure accompanying stress that those without pets.
- WebMD cites several studies that suggest that kids who grow up with a pet experience fewer problems with asthma and allergies. There are also indications that close contact with animals helps strengthen the immune system of infants and toddlers.
- A CDC study indicates that pet owners, particularly men, tend to have lower cholesterol and triglyceride levels than those who don't have pets.
- Walking your dog or playing fetch with him can also help keep you more active, keeping you in better physical shape.
- Marty Becker, a veterinary consultant for "Good Morning America", says that pets also help people suffering from chronic pain such as arthritis or migraine headaches. Pets reduce

anxiety and less anxiety tends to mean less pain. Some studies about acute pain indicate that adults using pet therapy required 50 percent less pain medication than those who did not.

- A 10-year study of 4300 Americans found that a cat in your home can cut the risk of a heart attack by almost one-third. Having a cat may also reduce the chance of a cardiovascular event like a stroke.
- The American Diabetes Association's magazine cited a 1992 study that found that one-third of the pets living with diabetics would change their behavior when their owner's blood sugar level dropped. That study has resulted in various organizations like Dogs4Diabetics training dogs as companions for patients with unstable blood glucose levels.
- Some studies also indicate that children who grow up in a household with pets learn to express themselves in more ways and relate better to others.

Choosing the Right Dog

Q: What are the most important things to keep in mind in choosing a shelter dog?
A: Look for a dog that fits with your lifestyle; do you want a small or large dog, one that's very active or laid-back, a playmate for your kids or a companion for yourself? If your shelter participates in the "Meet Your Match" program, fill out the questionnaire so shelter workers can point you toward some suitable matches. Once you've narrowed your choices to a few different dogs, spend a little time with each one so you can learn about that dog's personality. It's particularly important to get the dog out by himself if possible; many dogs behave much differently when they're not confined in a cage. And be sure to ask shelter workers about each dog you're interested in – why he's in the shelter, if he's been adopted out before and returned, what his medical history is, and so on. Most importantly, take your time – you're making a commitment that could last for 10 to 15 years or more and you owe it to the dog and to yourself to try to be sure you're making the right choice.

Q: I found a dog I like but he seems really keyed up – is that a problem?
A: Dogs that are kept cooped up most of the time in a cage can be full of energy when they're first let out. Be patient and give them a few minutes to burn off some of that excess energy. Once they calm down a little you can get a much better idea of what they are really like.

Q: What about the breed of dog?
A: Unless you have a particular breed or breeds in mind, do some homework before you go to the shelter. Learn a little bit about different breeds and their characteristics so you have a better idea of what you going to get from a particular shelter dog – remember even mixed breeds retain some of the traits of their parents. For example if you like a dog that's mostly border collie you should be aware that you're dealing with a high energy dog that not only wants to work but needs to work at something for at least four hours or so every day. With a Rottweiler you're getting a dog that needs to be brushed thoroughly at least once a week to get rid of the loose hair on his undercoat. And if you get a Lab mix – well, just be prepared for the kind of dog that has been known to get into his owner's car and go for a (short) drive on his own – in other words, a dog that needs close supervision.

Q: How can I tell if a particular dog at the shelter will get along with my dog(s) at home?
A: Many shelters have an area set aside where you can bring your dog or dogs to meet and get acquainted with your prospective adoptee.

Q: What are the most popular dog breeds?
A: According to the American Kennel Club the top 10 breeds in 2010 were:
1. Labrador Retriever
2. German Shepherd
3. Yorkshire Terrier
4. Beagle
5. Golden Retriever

6. Bulldog
7. Boxer
8. Dachshund
9. Poodle
10. Shih Tzu

Q: What are the most intelligent dog breeds?

A: According to most sources, the top 10 most intelligent breeds of dog are:
1. Border Collie
2. Poodle
3. German Shepherd
4. Golden Retriever
5. Doberman Pinscher
6. Shetland Sheepdog
7. Labrador Retriever
8. Papillon
9. Rottweiler
10. Australian Cattle Dog

Q: What things should you look for to see if a shelter dog is healthy?

A: There are several warnings signs to look for:
- A round or protruding stomach may indicate that the dog has worms (note: this is fairly common among pups and young dogs, and many shelters deworm their dogs as a standard procedure
- A dark red, crusty discharge in the ears indicates ear mites
- A runny nose or eyes could mean an upper respiratory infection
- A dull or patchy coat can be a sign of general poor health

Most of these problems are not serious and don't mean you have to cross the dog off your list; however each one requires some treatment and may take some time and money to get under control.

Q: How long do dogs live and which breeds live longest?
A: The median lifespan of all dogs is about 10 years, while the average lifespan for mixed breeds is about 11 years. In general smaller dogs tend to live longer than larger dogs, with very large dogs being considered "old" at 6 to 7 years of age. Dachshunds, Poodles and Shetland Sheepdogs tend to live the longest at 12 years or more, while Rottweilers, Greyhounds, and Irish Wolfhounds are usually the shortest lived breeds. And as with humans females tend to live a little longer than males. Here are average lifespans for a number of popular breeds:

- Labrador Retriever: 12.6 years
- Boxer: 10.4 years
- Doberman Pinscher: 9.8 years
- Border Collie: 13.0 years
- Golden Retriever: 12.0 years
- Cocker Spaniel: 12.5 years
- Chihuahua: 13.0 years
- Dalmation: 13.0 years
- Rottweiler: 9.8 years
- Beagle: 13.3 years
- Dachshund: 12.2 years
- Bulldog: 6.7 years
- Standard Poodle: 12.0 years
- Miniature Poodle: 14.8 years
- Pekingese: 13.3 years

- German Shepherd: 10.3 years
- Yorkshire Terrier: 12.8 years
- Great Dane: 8.4 years
- Weimaraner: 10.0 years

No matter which breed you pick (or if you choose a mixed breed), proper nutrition and exercise combined with regular visits to the veterinarian can help prolong any dog's life.

Author's note: Keep in mind that these are averages; I grew up with a dachshund who lived to be almost 17 years old.

Q: What are the general size categories for dogs?

A: Here's a suggested classification scheme by weight:
- Pocket (under 5 pounds)
- Toy (5 to 12 pounds)
- Miniature (13 to 25 pounds)
- Small (26 to 39 pounds)
- Medium (40 to 59 pounds)
- Large (60 to 79 pounds)
- Very Large (80 to 99 pounds)
- Giant (100 pounds and above)

Q: What breeds of dogs get along best with children?

A: This question will almost always start an argument among dog owners. People generally agree that Bulldogs, Collies, German Shepherds, Basset Hounds, Westies and a number of others usually get along great with kids. Beyond that you can get into some heated discussions about dogs like rottweilers and pit bulls. The fact is it depends a lot on a particular dog's age and personality, the age(s) of the children, and a number of factors other than dog breed.

There are a couple of things to keep in mind though. It's usually best to get a puppy that is at least 5 months old (that's roughly 10 years old in human years) so he's sturdy enough to handle normal play with kids. And try to find a dog that matches up well with your kid(s) - a large rambunctious dog may be a bit much for a 5 or 6 year old, but might be a perfect fit for an active 10 year old.

Q: What dogs are the easiest to train?
A: You can probably guess some of them; here's a partial list:
- Border Collie – maybe the easiest of all dogs to train
- German Shepherd
- Golden Retriever
- Standard Poodle
- Australian Shepherd
- Collie
- Miniature Schnauzer
- Weimaraner
- Pembroke Welsh Corgi
- Cocker Spaniel
- Shetland Sheepdog
- Labrador Retriever
- Doberman Pinscher

Keep in mind that female dogs are usually a little easier to train than males and that training needs to start at as early an age as possible.

Author's note: We have had a male Doberman, a male Lab, and a female Border Collie. Training the two males was somewhat of a struggle - the Doberman was good-natured but extremely hard-headed and the Lab was like an out-of-control teenager until he got to be about 3 years old. The Border Collie was my "once-in-a-lifetime" dog; she was full of life, very intelligent, and basically trained herself (you do have to find a "job" of some kind for your Border Collie though or she will find one on her own – and that's not a good thing).

Q: What breeds of dog don't shed a lot?
A: If you want to keep dog hair and dander to a minimum in your home or if you're allergic to animal dander, then one of the breeds below may be the one for you:
- Poodles (toy, miniature, and standard) – very little shedding although they all require regular grooming
- Schnauzer (standard, miniature or giant)
- Yorkshire terrier – these dogs lose very little hair, but have fairly high maintenance costs
- Bichon Frise – no undercoat and very few health problems
- Cairn terrier – small to medium size dogs, good with children
- Italian greyhound – very little shedding or dander

- West Highland White terrier (Westie) – medium size dogs
- American hairless terrier (toy, miniature and standard) – virtually no body hair

Q: What types of dog are best for families with young, active children who want to play with the dog?
A: Probably the best breeds for an active family are the pointers, retrievers, setters and spaniels. Keep in mind that there are also a lot of mixed breeds in shelters that could be a good fit.

Q: Are there certain breeds that don't get along with cats?
A: Dogs, like humans, are all individuals with their own particular personality; however there are some breeds that have an inherited impulse to chase and bring down small animals – like cats. Dog breeds with a high "prey drive" include:
- Afhgan Hound
- Akita
- Alaskan Malemute
- Australian Cattle Dog
- Basenji
- Beagle
- Border Collie
- Bull Mastiff
- Doberman Pinscher
- Greyhound
- Jack Russell Terrier
- Jindo
- Norwegian Elkhound
- Rhodesian Ridgeback

- Samoyed
- Siberian Husky
- Weimaraner
- Whippet
- Yorkshire Terrier

Author's note: Again, all dogs have their own personality. We have had a Doberman and a Border Collie and both of them lived for years with our cats and never showed the slightest inclination to attack any of them. The only problem we ever had was when our Border Collie as a pup made a couple of attempts to herd the cats – an attempt which the cats quickly discouraged. We did have a cat on our front porch that was mauled by a pair of Akitas that had gotten loose from their owner; but that appeared to be a case of the dogs trying to play, getting overly excited and the "prey drive" taking over.

Q: Are there certain breeds that tend to get along better with cats?
A: Dog breeds that tend to be more tolerant of cats include:
- Australian Shepard
- Boxer
- Cavalier King Charles spaniel
- Dachshund
- Dalmation
- Golden Retriever
- Labrador Retriever
- Maltese
- Papillon
- Pekingese

- Pomeranian
- Poodle
- Pug
- Shih Tzu
- Rottweiler

Q: I've heard certain dogs require a lot of grooming – what does grooming include?
A: Along with brushing and combing, grooming includes nail trimming, periodic baths, cleaning the eyes and ears, and even brushing the dog's teeth.

Q: What dogs require the most grooming?
A: These breeds require a good deal of grooming (brushing and combing every few days, regular baths and clipping about every 2 months):
- Airdale Terrier
- Bichon Frise
- Cavalier King Charles Spaniel
- English Springer Spaniel
- Irish Setter
- Maltese
- Schnauzer (all sizes)
- Poodle (all sizes)
- Newfoundland
- Old English Sheepdog
- Pekingese
- Saint Bernard
- Samoyed
- Scottish Terrier
- Yorkshire Terrier

These dogs require only moderate grooming (regular brushing and combing, bathing when necessary):
- Afghan Hound

- American Eskimo
- Basset Hound
- Border Collie
- Bull Mastiff
- Cairn Terrier
- Chesapeake Bay Retriever
- Shar-Pei
- Cocker Spaniel
- Collie
- Golden Retriever
- Lhasa Apso
- Pomeranian
- Rhodesian Ridgeback
- Saluki
- Shetland Sheepdog
- Siberian Husky
- Welsh Springer Spaniel
- West Highland White Terrier

And these breeds require very little grooming:
- Australian Shepherd
- Bloodhound
- Boston Terrier
- Bull Terrier
- Corgi
- Chow Chow
- Dalmatian
- Doberman Pinscher
- German Shepherd
- Great Dane
- Irish Wolfhound
- Labrador Retriever
- Mastiff
- Papillon
- Pointer

- Rottweiler
- Weimaraner
- Welsh Terrier

Q: Are there any dogs that require special care?
A: Hairless dogs like the Chinese Crested require sunscreen lotion before going out in direct sunlight

Q: Dogs that don't shed much don't need much grooming – right?
A: Not necessarily. Breeds like the poodle or Bichon Frise shed very little – but they require considerable grooming. On the other hand dogs like collies or huskies need very little grooming but shed heavily about twice a year.

Q: If I'm adopting a mixed breed puppy how can I tell how big he or she is going to be as an adult?
A: The people at the shelter can probably tell you or you can get a good idea from looking at the head and paws. If he has large paws or if his head is about as long as the rest of his body you can figure he's going to be a pretty big dog. Slender legs and small paws are a good indication that he's not going to grow a whole lot.

Pit Bull **Adoption**

Aren't pit bulls dangerous to humans and other pets?
The truth is that pit bulls, according to tests by the American Temperament Testing Society (ATTS) are no more dangerous than golden retrievers, beagles or any other popular breed. Like humans, every pit bull is an individual with its own personality but the vast majority of pit bulls, if properly raised, make excellent pets.

Q: But aren't pit bulls bred to be "fighting dogs"?
A: In the 1800s in England Olde English bulldogs were crossed with terriers to develop agile, aggressive dogs that were used for dog fighting. The "fighting instinct" though is a result of training methods that were used to reinforce and encourage the naturally somewhat aggressive nature of terriers. However even the pit bulls bred for fighting were selectively bred for bite inhibition toward humans so that their owners could handle them safely during fighting events. Properly socialized, current day pit bulls make loving pets and can coexist peacefully with dogs, cats, birds or other animals.

Q: Don't pit bulls have "locking jaws"?
A: No, there is nothing unusual about the structure of a pit bull's jaws. They do not "lock" onto things and refuse to let go till they tear it apart – that is a myth and part of the misinformation floating around about pit bulls.

Q: How can I tell if a particular dog is a pit bull?
A: There are certain characteristics identified with a pit bull, such as the somewhat blocky shape of the head. The truth is though that there is no specific breed known as "pit bulls". DNA tests have proven that dogs commonly identified as pit bulls are actually a mixture of different breeds.

43

Choosing the Right Cat

Q: I've never had a cat – what's it like living with a cat?

A: There are a number of things to keep in mind when you adopt a cat:

- Cats tend to be more independent than dogs; they generally DON'T come when called (unless there's food involved and sometimes not even then) and THEY choose when to get in your lap (or in your face)
- You need to keep the cat's litter box clean (scooped at least once a day and the litter changed every few days) – or your cat will find someplace else to do its business
- Be prepared for a certain amount of cat hair on the furniture (cats tend to completely disregard commands to stay off the furniture)
- Cats love to jump up on the counter or on a table and swat at objects until they knock them off onto the floor
- Cats tend to get hairballs on occasion causing them to throw up – usually on some important document that you left lying around
- Be aware that cats are also nocturnal – and they prefer to party along about 3 AM
- However you should also know that there is something very soothing about having a cat curl up on your lap or lie down next to you to take a nap – and after all, they ARE willing to let you admire them and cater to all their wants – what more could you ask?

Q: Can I find a purebred cat at a shelter?
A: These days less than 10 percent of all cats are purebreds; the rest are mixed breeds of various types. Your best bet if you're looking for a purebred cat is to find a reputable breeder. Be aware though that shelters offer a dazzling array of cats of every size, disposition and coloring you could imagine – and they make great pets even if they do have somewhat mixed parentage.

Q: Should I adopt an older cat?
A: For most people the natural inclination is to adopt a kitten; they are cute, cuddly and full of life. There are advantages though in adopting a cat that is already full grown:

- An adult cat's personality is fully developed, making it easier to find one that fits in with your life style
- A fully grown cat is most likely already litter trained
- Adult cats tend to be calmer and less likely to go bouncing around the house wreaking havoc
- With an fully grown cat you know what size cat you're getting
- And adult cats are the hardest to place – by adopting one you may truly be saving a life

Q: What are the most popular breeds of cat?
A: The Cat Fanciers' Association lists the following top 10 breeds for 2010:
1. Persian
2. Maine Coon
3. Exotic
4. Ragdoll

5. Sphynx
6. Siamese
7. Abyssinian
8. American Shorthair
9. Cornish Rex
10. Birman

Q: What are the most intelligent cat breeds?

A: Measuring the intelligence of a cat is considerably more subjective than rating the intelligence of dog breeds, but Animal Planet ranks them this way:

1. Sphynx
2. Balinese (essentially a long-haired Siamese)
3. Bengal
4. Colourpoint Shorthair (developed from Siamese and American and British Shorthairs)
5. Havana Brown (a cross of Siamese and black British or American Shorthairs)
6. Javanese (An Oriental Shorthair-Balinese cross)
7. Oriental (developed from numerous breeds including Siamese)
8. Siamese

Author's note: Keep in mind that in rating the intelligence of dogs or cats, you will often find mixed breed dogs or cats that can hold their own with any of the pure breeds.

Q: Which cats are the most sociable?

A: The more outgoing breeds of cats include:
- Balinese
- British Shorthair
- Burmese
- Himalayan

- Maine Coon
- Manx
- Persian
- Siamese
- Sphynx
- Tonkinese

Q: What are the most "doglike" cats?
A: Cats with doglike traits include:
- Burmese
- Cornish Rex
- Maine Coon
- Siberian

Q: What are some very active cat breeds?
A: If you're looking for a high-energy cat here are a few possibilities:
- Abyssinian
- Balinese
- Burmese
- Cornish Rex
- Javanese
- Siamese
- Siberian
- Sphynx
- Tonkinese

Q: Which cat is least likely to cause allergy problems?
A: The Siberian is probably the best choice for people who are allergic to animal dander.

Q: Which breeds are the most affectionate?

A: If you're looking for a cat that likes to curl up with you consider a cat that who is part or all:

- American Wirehair
- Balinese
- Burmese
- Cornish Rex
- Devon Rex
- Himalayan
- Javanese
- Maine Coon
- Manx
- Persian
- Siamese
- Sphynx
- Tonkinese

Keep in mind of course that every cat has its own personality; spending a little time getting to know a shelter cat is the best way to pick an affectionate companion.

Q: What if I want a cat who will talk with me?
A: The champion "talker" among cats has to be the Siamese (or any cat with a lot Siamese in his background). Siamese cats love to talk, sometimes to the point where you wish they would take a break for a few minutes. Siberian and Sphynx cats can also be good conversationalists.

Q: Which cats are the quietest?
A: On the average, the least demanding cat breeds include:

- Birman
- Himalayan
- Persian

- Russian Blue

Author's note: As always these are generalizations. We had a stray cat that was mostly Russian Blue and Ashley was always into something. So take all of these ratings with the proverbial grain of salt.

Q: Which cats are the longest-lived?
A: Lifespan isn't nearly as clear-cut with different breeds of cats (especially mixed breeds) as with dogs, but some research indicates that Siamese and Manx cats are among the longest-lived.

Author's note: We have had a number of mixed breed cats live to be 12 to 15 years old or more and we also had a Maine Coon that lived to be well over 20 years old.

Q: What things should I look for in evaluating a shelter cat?
A: Check the cat's eyes first – clear, bright eyes generally indicate a healthy cat. The nose should be clean and slightly moist, the ears should be clear of any discharge, and the coat should be clean, shiny and free of fleas (although it's difficult to keep all shelter animals flea-free). Listen to the cat's breathing too. Wheezing, coughing, sneezing or labored breathing can indicate some serious respiratory problems. Once you've picked out a couple of possible adoptees, try playing with each one and see what kind of personality they have.

Author's note: Several years ago my younger daughter rescued a kitten from the pound that had some discharge from her eyes. We checked with our veterinarian for advice about the eye discharge before we adopted and found out that it was a minor problem – a little medication cleared it up within a couple of weeks and the kitten has grown into a healthy, happy cat. You don't necessarily have to write off a cat that you like because of one item that needs treatment.

Cat Behavior

Q: Why do cats rub up against everything?
A: Cats have scent glands on each side of their head, on their lips and chin, along the tail and at the base of their tail and they use those glands to mark their territory. When a cat rubs up against you or the furniture or a doorway it's marking that thing as "his" or "hers". Rubbing against things is OK – what you don't want to see is spraying (urinating on different things in the house) which is also a means of marking territory. Fortunately cats brought up in a home environment usually don't spray inside the house, although a few do start to do so as they get older.

Q: Why does a cat "knead"?
A: When a kitten is nursing it kneads its paws against the mother to encourage milk flow and as a sign of contentment. When a grown cat kneads it is simply a sign of pleasure and contentment.

Q: Why does a cat butt its head against you?
A: Pushing its head against you is a cat's way of showing affection.

Q: Why does a cat sometimes lick its fur right after being petted?
A: There are two theories about this – either the cat is trying to get rid of your smell or it is tasting your scent – take your pick.

Q: Why do cats always seem to go to visitors who don't like cats?

A: One explanation is that when one cat doesn't like another cat, it faces it head on, spits and hisses and often moves toward the other cat. People who don't like cats tend to avoid looking at them or talking to them and the cat interprets that as being "cat friendly". Another explanation is that cats just love to torture people who don't properly appreciate cats.

Q: Why does a cat sometimes scratch next to his food dish as if he's trying to bury it?

A: Either it's a throwback to cats in the wild burying food for later … or he's telling you that you should bury that bunch of cat food and get something better.

Q: Why does a cat sometimes make a face like he's sneering when smelling something?

A: When a cat does this it's because he has discovered an interesting odor and is smelling it more deeply. Called "flehming" it draws the odor into an organ (Jacobson's organ) in the roof of the cat's mouth.

Q: Does a cat scratch a piece of furniture to sharpen his claws?

A: It's more likely that he is marking his territory. Cats have sweat glands between their paw pads and scratching leaves their scent on the object they're clawing.

Q: Why do cats turn over the water bowl?

A: Cats don't like to drink out of bowls that are small enough that their whiskers touch the sides of the bowl.

Q: Why does a cat "chatter" while it's watching a bird outside?
A: When a cat kills prey he bites down rapidly several times. By "chattering" the cat is imitating its behavior if it was actually attacking the bird. Note: some experts feel that the chattering is more a sign of the cat's frustration at not being able to get at the bird.

Dog Behavior

Q: Why do dogs love to chase things?
A: It's called "prey drive". Prey drive is the instinctual urge to chase down small animals and kill them for food. In domesticated dogs the urge is more involved with just chasing down and retrieving the stick or ball. In fact the name "ball drive" is even used at times in discussing the urge dogs have to chase balls.

Author's note: Chasing a ball may also be a substitute for some other behavior. I had a female border collie and, as anyone who has had a border collie knows, they have to have a "job" to work at each day. When Abby figured out that we didn't want her herding the cats she picked playing ball as her "job".

Q: Why do dogs want to get on your bed?
A: Your bed smells more strongly of you than anyplace else in the house and your dog enjoys being close to you (or at least to your scent). That may be flattering, but experts warn that letting your dog sleep on the bed with you can lead to problems if the dog decides the bed is his domain. If your dog is large and likes to stretch out it can also lead to you finding yourself teetering on the edge of the bed as your dog slowly pushes you off onto the floor.

Q: Why do dogs sometimes roll in really foul smelling stuff?

A: Animal behaviorists say that it's a throwback to their ancestors who had to hunt for their food. Rolling in strong smelling things gives predators an advantage because their scent is masked from the animals they're hunting.

Q: Why do dogs like to lift their leg and pee on a tree or bush?
A: They are putting their scent at nose level so other dogs can smell it more easily.

Q: Why do dogs eat poop?
A: It's in their genes. Dogs were originally scavengers and lived off of whatever edible foodstuffs they could find, including the waste from other animals. Even now females normally eat the poop of their newborn pups in order to keep the nest clean.

Q: If a dog is wagging his tail does that mean he's friendly?
A: Not necessarily. Rapid tail wagging can also be a sign of aggressiveness.

Q: Why do dogs pant when they're hot?
A: When a dog gets hot blood flow to the tongue increases, making it bigger. The dog will stick his tongue out and take quick, short breaths to make saliva evaporate and help cool himself.

Q: Can dogs see in color?
A: Yes, to a point. Normal humans have three types of color receptors – red, green and blue. Dogs don't have the receptors for the color green, which means they have trouble distinguishing between greenish-

yellow, orange, and red. They have a form of colorblindness called deuteranopia and can't tell red from green – just another reason to never let your dog try to drive.

Q: Why do dogs have whiskers?
A: Whiskers serve as an early warning device for dogs. They tell him is something is near his face and help keep him from colliding with walls and other objects. They may also help him decide whether or not he can safely enter a closed space - if his whiskers don't touch the sides of the enclosed area he can be pretty sure he'll fit inside and not get stuck.

Keeping Your Pet Safe

Q: What if my pet gets lost?
A: The best way to make sure your dog or cat gets returned safely if it gets lost is to make sure it's wearing a collar and current id tags and to have it microchipped. In fact microchipping is the best way to protect your pet since a dog or cat can slip out of a collar, while a microchip is a permanent means of identification.

Microchipping is a simple and inexpensive process. The veterinarian or an assistant injects a chip about the size of a grain of rice under the pet's skin between the shoulder blades. It only takes a few seconds and is no more painful than a routine shot. A veterinarian or an animal shelter can do a quick scan of an implanted microchip and immediately find out the owner's name, address and phone number.

Q: Should I let my cat go outside?
A: If at all possible keep your cat indoors. Indoor cats live longer, stay safer and healthier. A fenced yard isn't much of a barrier to a cat and outside hazards can include cars, storm drains, roaming dogs, and even animal thieves (who grab and sell cats for profit).

Q: What if my dog is outside and starts to run into the street?
A: If your dog is outside of a fenced yard the safest thing is to keep him on a leash. Failing that, make sure your dog is trained to obey simple commands

like sit, stay, and stop – commands that could save his life.

Q: What about letting other pets come around my dog or cat?
A: Just use common sense and if another animal is extremely aggressive be very careful about letting him around your pet. Or if an animal's eyes are cloudy or runny, or he is wheezing or snorting continuously, or he has one or more patches of fur missing, it's a good idea to keep your pet away from him. And where dogs are concerned, if you have a small dog (or cat) be familiar with dogs who have a strong prey instinct and avoid them.

Q: Is it OK to toss my dog into the water when we're out on the lake?
A: Aside from the fact that your dog may not particularly enjoy an impromptu bath, not all dogs can swim. Some breeds like basset hounds and bulldogs have the swimming ability of a cement block. thers, like Greyhounds, Pugs, Dachshunds and Westies are known to have trouble swimming. In fact there's no guarantee that any particular dog can manage if just tossed in the water. And even good swimmers can get in serious trouble if they don't know where to go to get out of the water.

Q: What if it's hot outside and I have to leave my pet in the car while I run into the store?
A: The simple answer is – Do NOT leave your dog or cat locked up in a hot car. Realistically there may be a time when you do need to do just that. Remember to crack the windows so a little air can flow through and try to park where part of the car is in the shade.

And don't leave your pet in the car in direct sun for more than 10 or 15 minutes. If you've got your pet with you in the car in hot weather it's also a good idea to keep one of those collapsible bowls and a bottle of water in the car so your pet can get a drink if necessary.

Q: What precautions should I take if my dog is outside during hot weather?
A: Make sure that there is shade and some cool, clean water available if your dog is outside in the heat of the day. Dogs do sweat (through the pads of their feet) but their cooling system isn't nearly as efficient as a human's. Don't exercise your dog while it's hot and if your dog is big and/or has a heavy coat (or undercoat) only let him out in the heat for short periods of time.

If you've ever heard the old saw that a horse won't go where it's liable to fall – not true. And dogs don't instinctively know when they're getting too hot. You have to keep a close eye on them and watch for signs such as excessive panting, dizziness or disorientation, thick saliva, or a dark red color to the gums. If your dog is showing signs of heat stroke get him out of the heat and use cool, wet (NOT icy cold) wash rags to cool him down slowly.

Q: What about cold weather safety for pets?
A: Dogs and cats have a higher internal temperature than humans and they have a fur coat, so they tend to handle cold fairly well. However, if your pet is outside in the cold for any considerable length of time, unless he's a Huskie or Malamute, you should have a heated shelter of some kind available for him.

Small dogs or dogs with very short coats should have sweaters or jackets for protection from the cold, if the dog will tolerate clothing.

Cats should only be allowed outside in winter weather for short periods if at all. They tend to go off on their own which means you may be going in and out for hours waiting for them to show up again so you can get them back inside.

Avoid letting your dog eat snow – there could be chemicals or sharp object mixed into the snow. And try to keep him from running on ice; dogs may have four legs but they can fall and get hurt just the same as humans. Finally, look for signs of developing hypothermia: excessive shaking or shivering, sluggishness, or lying down in the snow and not moving.

Author's note: There are exceptions to every rule – Rottweilers are supposed to be somewhat vulnerable to cold but Jade, our Rottie, used to love to go out and lie in the snow for an hour or more at a time. In some cases you just have to find out how your particular pet reacts to heat or cold.

Keeping Your Pet Healthy

Q: What should I feed my dog?
A: That depends on a number of things: your dog's age, physical condition, lifestyle, and to some extent, your budget. Dogs that spend a lot of time outdoors and get a lot of exercise are going to need more calories than one that spends most of the day lying around the house. And dogs in cold weather areas may need more fat in their diet to keep them warm when they're outside.

Whatever dog food you choose, the first thing listed in the ingredients should be a meat such as chicken or lamb – not just "meat meal", which can include almost anything. If the food contains by-products (and almost all of them do) make sure the by-product meal is specific such as lamb or chicken by-products and not just listed as "poultry", "meat", or "animal".

In case you're interested, meat by-products include organ matter such as the liver, spleen, lungs, heart, brains, intestines, stomach, etc. - but not hair, teeth, feathers, or hooves. Although the thought of eating those items may be slightly repulsive to us, they are actually very high in natural vitamins and minerals.

Some dog foods also use corn (which is a protein source) as a filler. Some dogs don't have any problem with corn, but some do. If you see your dog licking his feet, scratching, or scooting on his butt it could be a sign that he's allergic to corn. Wheat can also cause a similar allergic reaction and so can soy.

[Author's note: We've had two dogs that were allergic to corn – changing to a dog food without corn solved the problem in both cases.]

You should also avoid foods that use chemical preservatives like BHA, BHT, or propyl gallate.

Q: How often should I feed my dog?
A: Puppies should be fed three times a day until they're about 4 months old; then you can switch to twice-a-day feedings. Adult dogs should normally be fed twice a day. Note: Just as with humans, there is some research that indicates that a number of small feedings during the day may be even better for helping your dog to maintain a healthy weight (although for most of us who work, multiple feedings during the day are probably not practical).

Q: Can I feed my puppy regular dog chow?
A: Puppies need about twice as many calories per pound as an adult dog so you should stick to special "puppy" formula foods for the first six months or so.

Q: Should I feed my dog dry chow or canned dog food?
A: Given the same nutritional value it doesn't really matter which you choose. Dry dog food costs less per serving and it's more concentrated which means you'll need to feed less. Dogs with urinary tract or dental problems may do better on semi-moist or canned dog food which contain anywhere from 10 to 75 percent more moisture than dry dog food. Also

canned dog food lets you serve a bigger helping for the same amount of calories as in dry dog food which can help your dog to feel like he's had more to eat.

Q: I want to change my dog's food – should I just start him on the new food all at once?
A: It's a good idea to mix the new food in gradually with the old dog food to give your dog's system time to adjust to the change in diet.

Q: How do I know if I'm overfeeding or underfeeding my dog?
A: If you can't feel your dog's ribs or you can't see a waist behind the ribs then you're overfeeding; if you can see his ribs, backbone and pelvic bones and can't feel any fat over the bones then you're underfeeding.

Q: Should I feed my dog table food?
A: The food you eat will nourish your dog the same as it does you. However, you need to keep the quantities small and avoid food with seasonings, sauces, or butter. The advantage to dog foods like kibbles versus table food is that the dog food is nutritionally balanced to provide the right number of calories to your pet. It's also a good idea to feed your dog vegetables on occasion; for example green beans make a good low-calorie snack for your dog.

Just make sure that you don't give your dog grapes, raisins, chocolate, avacados, garlic, onions, milk or large amounts of bread. All these food are potentially dangerous to your pet and should be avoided.

Q: Where can I find more information on what to feed my dog or cat?

A: There are several websites you can go to for more information about your pet's diet:

- www.petdiets.com
- http://www.aspca.org/Home/Pet-care.aspx
- www.petsmart.com
- www.dogbreedinfo.com/feeding.htm
- www.2ndchance.info/dogfood.htm
- www.2ndchance.info/catfood.htm

Plus you can find a number of good books dealing with what to feed your pet:

- "Home-Prepared Dog & Cat Diets: The Healthful Alternative" by Donald Strombeck
- "The Whole Pet Diet: Eight Weeks to Great Health for Dogs and Cats" by Andi Brown and Richard Pitcairn

Q: How often should I change my pet's water?

A: You wouldn't want to drink stale water – change your pet's water at least once a day and keep the water bowl full. And if you keep a large container of water outside be sure you empty and refill it every day or two as well – drinking stagnant water can be dangerous to your pet's health.

Q: Do I need to brush my dog's teeth?

A: You should either have your veterinarian clean your dog's teeth on a fairly regular basis or do it yourself. Clean the teeth with dog toothpaste or a baking-soda-and-water paste using a dog toothbrush or a gauze pad.

Q: What about vaccinations?
A: Puppies should be vaccinated with a combination vaccine at 2, 3, and 4 months of age and then once a year. This vaccine protects against parvovirus, distemper, hepatitis, parainfluenza and leptospirosis. Kittens should receive a vaccination for feline panleukopenia (FPV), feline calicivirus (FCV), feline rhinotracheitis (FHV), and Chlamydia psittaci (CP) at about 7 to 9 weeks of age. Kittens should also be given booster shots at 12-13 weeks and again at 16-18 weeks of age, along with a vaccination for feline leukemia (FLV) and for rabies. For adult dogs and cats, consult your veterinarian about a schedule for booster vaccinations.

Q: What kind of grooming does my dog need?
A: There are just a few simple things you should do to keep your dog well groomed:

- Give your dog a bath regularly using shampoo and conditioner made especially for dogs. Be sure to rinse thoroughly to get all the soap off – soapy residue can dry out your dog's skin.
- Keep the toenails clipped. More active dogs may keep their nails worn down just by exercising, but be sure not to let the nails get overly long. Be careful not to trim the nails too short or you can cut into the quick and cause some bleeding and discomfort.
- Brush your dog periodically; even dogs with very short coats can shed and leave a considerable amount of hair around. Just how often and how much time you need to spend brushing depends on the dog. Dogs with a

thick undercoat require at least once a week brushing.
- Keep your dog's ears clean. Use ear cleaner from the pet store – put a small amount on a cotton ball and swab the outer surface of the inner ear.

Q: What about fleas and ticks?
A: Check your pet at least every few days during the summer for fleas and ticks.

Q: Are some household plants poisonous to cats?
A: There are a number of popular houseplants that are poisonous to cats including:
- Arrowhead fern
- Boston Ivy
- Cactus
- Caladium
- Chrysanthemum
- Crocus
- Daffodil
- Diffenbachia
- Holly
- Hydrangea
- Lily
- Mistletoe
- Philodendron
- Tomato leaves

Q: How can I keep my cats away from our houseplants?
A: There are several non-toxic substances you can spray on plant leaves to make them smell or taste

terrible to your cats. Bitter Apple is one repellent that's safe for your plants and is usually available in pet supply stores. Or if your plant is in a medium-to-large container, placing sharp rocks on top of the soil will tend to discourage your cat from sitting there and chewing on the plant.

Q: Should I take my dog to a dog park?

A: Dog parks can be great – they give your pooch a chance to run and play and to socialize with other dogs and their owners. However, even if you go to a dog park that has strict rules about allowing only dogs that have been spayed or neutered, are non-aggressive, are current on their vaccinations and do not have any health problems, there are still people who will disregard those rules. There's always the risk of your dog getting bitten or catching something like kennel cough – and that can mean a fair-sized vet bill.

Q: What is pet insurance and do I need it?

A: For most of us who have pets, one of the really gut-wrenching moments is when you find out that your pet has a serious medical problem and you have to decide how much your pet's life is worth. Of course the first impulse is to pay whatever it costs to fix the problem – but what if it runs into hundreds or even thousands of dollars? That's were pet insurance comes in.

Pet insurance is a policy that covers your dogs, cats, birds or whatever as long as they're healthy. If there's a medical emergency you only pay the deductible, not the entire bill. Insurance policies of this type often cover kenneling, travel and other costs in addition to veterinary bills. Like other policies, pet insurance comes in multiple levels, which vary based on price and deductible amounts.

You should review policy options for things such as vet fees, accidental damage, theft or straying, third party liability and legal expenses, and boarding kennel expenses. It's also best to insure pets by the time they're six months old; the longer you wait the more difficult it is to get them insured.

Health Issues

Q: What is the most common health problem for dogs and cats?
A: Several recent surveys indicate that the most common health problem for pets in the United States is obesity. According to one study over half the dogs and cats in the U.S. are overweight and obesity can lead to any number of complications. To make matters worse, the majority of pet owners don't even realize that their dog or cat is overweight.

Signs of obesity in dogs include the ribs becoming more difficult to feel, the waist beginning to disappear and the abdominal tuck becoming less defined. In cats the abdominal fat pad starts to increase in size and the waist starts to disappear. In more advanced cases fat deposits may become visible on the back and at the base of the tail.

Obesity usually results from overfeeding, improper diet, lack of exercise or hormonal imbalance.

Q: Are some foods dangerous for dogs or cats to eat?
A: There are a number of foods that can be extremely dangerous to your dog or cat:
- Grapes – grapes can make dogs sick and eventually lead to kidney failure.
- Chocolate – most pet owners already know to keep chocolate away from their dog – chocolate in any form can be poisonous and even fatal if your dogs get hold of it.

- Caffeine – Caffeine in even small doses (such as a small cup of coffee) can be fatal to both dogs and cats.
- Raw meat – Dogs are just as susceptible to salmonella and e coli as humans. Make sure any meat they eat has been cooked.
- Onions, avacados and garlic – A small amount of any of these items can cause anemia or strong allergic reactions.

Q: Can dogs or cats get diabetes?
A: Dogs and cats suffer from diabetes mellitus the same as humans. Diabetes mellitus is a disease of the endocrine gland system – specifically the pancreas, which regulates the dog or cat's blood sugar level. There are 2 types of diabetes mellitus: type 1 which is caused by a deficiency of insulin, the hormone that regulates how sugar is absorbed and utilized, and type 2 which is caused by a failure of the body's cells to utilize insulin properly.

Diabetes in dogs is usually type 1, in cats it is usually type 2 diabetes. The main factors that influence a pet's susceptibility to diabetes are its weight and its genetics. Being overweight can make a dog or cat more susceptible, plus certain breeds seem to be more at risk, including toy and miniature poodles, Dachsunds, Westies, Pugs, miniature Schnauers, and Burmese cats. Some breeds like Golden Retrievers and German Shepherds rarely develop the disease.

Diabetes usually occurs in dogs and cats somewhere between 7 and 10 years old. Unfortunately it normally develops gradually is easily missed until it gets to an advanced stage. First indications may be that the dog or cat is drinking excessively and urinating very frequently. Cataracts and general malaise are also common signs in dogs.

If you suspect a pet has diabetes, a simple test by your veterinarian that involves measuring blood fructosamine levels can help detect it. Treatment usually involves administering insulin shots and keeping to a carefully controlled diet.

Authors note: Our family has had two pets that contracted diabetes mellitus – a miniature poodle and a mixed breed cat. Insulin shots and a special diet helped control the disease in both cases, but you should always keep a close eye on a pet with diabetes since their condition can deteriorate rapidly.

Q: What is hip dysplasia?
A: Hip dysplasia is primarily a canine disease. It is caused by an abnormal formation of the hip that leads to looseness in the hip joints which in turn causes cartilage damage. At that point progressive arthritis can set in, which can be crippling.

Hip dysplasia is passed on genetically and is the most common in larger dogs, especially Rottweilers, Labrador Retrievers, Golden Retrievers, German Shepherds, Mastiffs and Saint Bernards. Smaller breeds like Cocker Spaniels, Pugs and mixed breeds can also develop hip dysplasia. Warning signs include difficulty getting up, lameness in the rear legs, reluctance to jump up, and a decreased activity level in general.

There are two options for treatment; surgical and non-surgical. Non-surgical methods include pain medication, weight loss diets, controlled exercise and physical therapy. These treatments generally have limited success. The other option is surgery and there are several types of surgery in use, including total hip replacement. If your pet is suffering from hip dysplasia, your veterinarian can suggest the best treatment options. Note: If possible you should look into pet insurance to help financially with situations like this that may require expensive procedures.

Q: Is cancer a common problem in dogs and cats?
A: Unfortunately cats and dogs are just as likely to develop cancer as humans – in fact cancer is the leading cause of death in dogs and cats. Just as with humans early diagnosis and treatment greatly improves the chances of survival. Some common signs of cancer:

- Abnormal swellings that persist or continue to grow
- Sores that don't heal
- Loss of appetite and/or increased water intake
- Weight loss
- Bleeding or discharge from any body opening
- Reluctance to exercise, loss of stamina
- Difficulty eating or swallowing
- Increased urination
- Abnormal breathing

Q: What about dental care?

A: One of the most common ailments in both cats and dogs is dental disease. Plaque buildup on teeth leads to red, irritated gums (a condition call gingivitis) and over time plaque can destroy the bone that holds the tooth in place. In some instances bacteria can even get into the bloodstream leading to serious infections in the heart, kidney, or liver.

Cleaning the teeth on a regular basis and feeding a balanced diet of dry chow can help prevent plaque buildup. If possible brush your pet's teeth regularly with a toothpaste made for pets (human toothpaste if swallowed can irritate your pet's stomach). Nylon bones and chew toys can also help stimulate the gums and scrape away plaque.

Q: What is heartworm disease and do I need to give my pet heartworm medicine?
A: Heartworm disease is a potentially fatal condition in dogs and cats caused by parasitic worms living in the arteries around the lungs or in the heart. Heartworm disease is spread by mosquitoes infected with heartworm larvae. The infected mosquitoes bite an animal and the larvae enter through the bite wound, make their way into the arteries and in about six months they mature into adult worms. The adult worms begin to clog and damage the arteries which eventually leads to aneurysms, abnormal blood clotting (embolisms), pulmonary hypertension and heart failure.

Heartworm disease may not be noticeable in its early stages and even animals that are heavily infected may only seem to tire more easily and have less of an appetite than usual. Treating heartworm disease in dogs is complicated and expensive and there is not effective treatment for cats. Fortunately prevention is safe, easy and inexpensive. There are several options for preventing heartworms, including daily or monthly tablets, topical creams and a six month shot (for dogs only).

Q: What is "kennel cough"?
A: Kennel cough is a highly contagious viral or bacterial infection that causes inflammation of the upper respiratory system. It's similar to a chest cold in humans and causes a dry, hacking cough. The dog usually appears perfectly healthy except for the persistent cough, which gets worse after exercise or if the dog is excited. Kennel cough normally clears up on its own after 3 or 4 weeks – however it's a good idea to have the dog checked by a veterinarian, plus the vet can prescribe a cough suppressant. Also, if you have other dogs in the household it's a good bet that they will also get infected since kennel cough is so highly contagious. If the dog refuses to eat and seems lethargic get him to a veterinarian immediately; in severe cases kennel cough can lead to pneumonia.

Q: There are worms in my pet's poop – what does that mean?
A: It means that your pet has intestinal parasites. Intestinal worms in cats and dogs live in the digestive tract, causing damage and robbing your pet of needed nutrients. The four common intestinal worms in dogs and cats are roundworms, whipworms, tapeworms, and hookworms. If you see worms in your pet's feces take a sample of the poop

to your veterinarian. Your vet can examine the sample, identify the type or worms and prescribe medication to clear up the infection. Be aware that once the medication starts to work you will still see some worms in the pet's feces for a day or two as the worms are eliminated. Note: intestinal worms in your pet aren't normally a threat to humans, but in some cases hookworm larvae in the soil can penetrate a person's skin and produce an itchy rash.

Q: What do I do if my dog keeps shaking his head and scratching at his ear?
A: If the dog tries to scratch whenever you touch his ear and you can see a dark, crumbly material inside the ear the odds are that he has ear mites (tiny spiderlike creatures that live inside the ear). Pet stores carry a wide variety of ear mite medicines or your veterinarian my prescribe an ointment containing nemycin sulfate that will kill the mites and soothe the inflammation inside the ear.

Q: Will spaying or neutering help keep my pet healthy?
A: Spaying (removal of the ovaries and uterus) can help reduce the risk of breast cancer and eliminate the chance of an infected uterus. Even more important, it protects your female from having unwanted litters. Neutering males (removal of the testicles) prevents testicular and prostate diseases, as well as some hernias. Neutering can also act to decrease aggressiveness in males. Note: spaying and neutering should be done by six months of age.

Q: Won't spaying or neutering make my pet gain weight?

A: No – spaying and neutering do not make pets fat. Overeating and insufficient exercise are the main causes of weight gain and lack of muscle tone.

Q: What do I do if my dog is overweight?

A: First, be sure the food you're giving him is reasonably fresh and nutritious. Low quality commercial foods that don't deliver enough nutrition can keep your dog feeling hungry and continually asking for more to eat. If you're satisfied with what you're feeding him, try cutting down on the amount of food at each meal by about 25 percent and supplement his diet with cooked rice or vegetables. Most people feed their dogs twice a day – once in the morning and once in the early evening – but you can also try feeding more often and using smaller amounts. Also, if your dog eats too fast and gulps his food, you can try packing the food into a kong toy to force him to eat slower.

Q: What do I do if I have a dog or cat about to give birth?

A: In most cases dogs and cats should be spayed or neutered to avoid this particular problem. However, if you find out that your pet is pregnant and close to term or if you find a stray that is about to give birth, there are some basic steps to remember to help with labor and delivery:

- A whelping (dog) or queening (cat) box should be provided for the mother to sleep in so that you know where the puppies or kittens will be born. The box should be relatively small with

6 to 8 inch high sides to keep the newborns from crawling out. If possible put the box in a place that's familiar to the mother but somewhat out of the way. Fill the box with newspaper or other bedding and change the bedding frequently.

- Stage 1 labor – During the first stage of labor the mother usually seems nervous and restless and may refuse to eat anything. This stage normally lasts from 6 to 24 hours.
- Stage 2 labor – Contractions and actual birthing begin. First a small greenish sac of fluid protrudes from the vulva, followed by a fetus and the attached placenta. Normal presentation is nose first, stomach down although it's also common to have some come newborns come out hind quarters first. After delivery the mother opens the sac, cleans off the puppies or kittens and severs the umbilical cord. In some cases you may have to do those things for the mother.
- Stage 3 labor – A resting stage between each delivery. Mild contractions and delivery of the afterbirth are part of this stage, which usually lasts 10 to 30 minutes (although it can be anywhere from a few seconds to an hour or more).
- Additional steps – If the mother fails to do so, remove all membranes covering the newborn, clean the face, and remove mucus from the mouth and nose. Rub the kitten or puppy with a clean towel to stimulate respiration – after a few minutes of rubbing the newborn should start to squirm and cry loudly. Make sure to

tie the umbilical cord about an inch from the body with fine thread.

Note: If a fetus Is lodged in the birth canal, take a clean towel and pull gently, applying steady pressure. If you still can't move the fetus you need to get the mother to a veterinarian as quickly as possible.

Medication and First Aid

Note: This is just a small sample of the type of situations you may have to deal with as far as providing immediate first aid or medicating your pet; in all cases if you have a sick or injured animal you should contact your veterinarian as soon as possible to make sure your pet gets the proper medical treatment. For more in depth and detailed information on medical care for your pet keep a book like "The First Aid Companion for Dogs & Cats" (by Amy D. Shojai) or "Pet First Aid: Cats and Dogs" (by the American Red Cross) handy or go to a website such as http://pet.justanswer.com where you can consult with a veterinarian online.

Q: My pet swallowed some cleaning fluid and I can't get hold of a veterinarian?
A: If you're sure your pet has swallowed a poisonous substance and you can't get in touch with a veterinarian, you call the Animal Poison Control Center at 888-426-4435 anytime, night or day (Note: there is a consultation fee).

Q: If my pet has swallowed a toxic product of some kind what do I need to take along to the vet?
A: Bring the product container or packaging and if your pet has vomited, place that in a plastic bag and bring it along too.

Q: How do I keep an injured dog or cat from biting me?

A: Even the gentlest animal may bite when it is injured and in pain. To protect yourself you should always muzzle the animal before doing anything else. If you don't have a muzzle handy improvise one using a necktie or a long stocking; tie a loop in it and slip it over the dog's nose. Tighten the knot, slip the ends under the nose and tie a second knot, then pull the rest of the ends over his neck and tie a third knot to hold the makeshift muzzle in place.

Cats and dogs have such short snouts that a muzzle isn't really practicable. In that case you can try to slip a bag or pillowcase completely over the animal's head and hold it in place. Cats are notoriously hard to restrain and tend to strongly resist having anything put over their head, so a better option may be to buy a cat muzzle and keep it handy.

When using a muzzle make sure the nostrils aren't covered and be ready to remove the muzzle immediately if the animal begins to vomit or is obviously having difficulty breathing.

Q: How do you perform CPR on a pet?

A: Performing CPR on a dog or cat is very similar to doing CPR on a human. First of all try to make sure the animal has actually stopped breathing; check for rise and fall of the chest, feel for breath on your palm, and look for the tell-tale blue color of the gums. Once you're sure your pet isn't breathing, open the pet's mouth and check to make sure the airway is clear. If the airway is blocked grab the tongue and pull it outward to dislodge the object or reach in with your fingers or small pliers and grab it. If you can't get hold of the object use the Heimlich maneuver.

Once the airway is clear lay the pet on its side, lift the chin and close the mouth with one or both hands to seal it. Put your mouth completely over the animal's nose and blow with two quick breaths, watching to see if the lungs expand. Continue, giving 15 to 20 breaths per minute until the pet begins to breath on its own or you reach the veterinarian.

If the heart has stopped you will also need to alternate breathing with chest compressions. You can hold your palm flat against the lower chest directly behind the left front elbow to feel for a heartbeat or you can try to find a pulse in the femoral artery on the inside of the thigh at the groin. Place your fingers flat against this area, press firmly and you should feel a pulse.

To do chest compressions for an animal under 20 pounds place the pet on his side on a relatively flat surface and cup your hand over the chest just behind the elbows. Squeeze firmly pressing in about ½ inch, with your thumb on one side and your fingers on the other. For animals over 20 pounds place one hand on top of the other against the chest and push down 25 to 50 percent.

Q: What's the best way to put medicine in a pet's ears?
A: Pets ear canals are long and curving, so tilt your pet's head so the opening of the ear points upward,

then put several drops of the medicine in the ear canal. Press the earflap down to make sure he doesn't shake his head and send the medicine flying and massage the base of the ear with your other hand.

Q: How do I put medicine in my pet's eyes?
A: Tip your pet's head back so he's looking upward and gently pull down the lower eyelid. Drip or squirt several drops of medicine onto the cupped tissue of the lower eyelid. Release the eyelid and let your pet blink several times; the medicine will spread over the surface of the eye as he blinks.

Q: How do I get my pet to take a pill?
A: There are techniques you can use to get your pet to swallow a pill, but the easiest way is to wrap the pill in a treat of some kind (like a small piece of cheese). If the pill is very large, try crushing it and mixing it into a bite of some (preferably strong-smelling) cat or dog food. If you have to do it by hand, consider using a pill syringe (available at most pet supply stores).

Q: What if my has burned his paws on a hot asphalt road?
A: Put you pet's feet in cold water immediately. Spray or soak his feet for at least 5 to 10 minutes. Have him stand in a roasting pan filled with cold water, or if you have a cat that refuses to get into the water, use a cold compress (either a coldpack or a washcloth filled with ice).

Q: My pet's feet have been burned by road salt – what should I do?
A: For chemical burns flood his paws with cool to lukewarm water for at least 20 minutes.

Q: What should I do if my pet is bleeding?
A: Don't wash the wound if it's bleeding heavily – it will make it harder for a clot to form. Apply a gauze pad or clean piece of cloth to the wound and put pressure on it. If blood soaks through put a second pad on top of the first and continue to apply pressure. If you can't stop the bleeding by pressing with your hand wrap the gauze pad in several layers of roll gauze and cover that with an elastic bandage like an Ace bandage or even duct tape. Make the bandage firm but not too tight. Bleeding should stop within 5 minutes or less – if not, take your pet to a veterinarian immediately.

Q: My pet's stomach is distended, his gums are pale and he seems weak – what's wrong?
A: He may be suffering from bloat – a condition where the stomach swells and may become twisted. Bloat is potentially life-threatening. Wrap him in a warm blanket and take him to your vet right away.

Miscellaneous

Q: How old is my pet in human terms?
A: The classic answer is that each year a dog ages is like seven years for a human. A somewhat more accurate rule is that a 1 year old dog is equivalent to a 15 year old human, a 2 year old dog would be about 24 in human years and then each additional year a dog ages is equal to 4 years of human life.

Q: What's the maximum life span for a dog or cat?
A: The official record for the longest lived dog is 29 years, although obviously record-keeping of this type is sketchy at best. Cats have also been known to live well over 20 years. (Author's note: we had a Maine Coon cat that according to the veterinarian's best estimate was about 28 years old when he passed away).

Q: I want to put a dog house in the back yard – what features should I look for in a dog house?
A: The dog house should be large enough for your dog to turn around in and to stretch out full length. It should have ventilation of some type and should be insulated if possible. A raised floor is also a good idea to help keep water out and to keep the house warmer in winter and cooler in summer.

Q: Do dogs and cats have the same emotions as humans?
A: Well, after years of exhaustive study experts at the Tufts School of Medicine have determined what

pet owners already knew - that dogs and cats do experience fear, sadness, anger, happiness, jealousy and even embarrassment (if you don't believe animals get embarrassed, watch a cat that has just tried to jump on a counter and fell off – they all have that "I meant to do that" look).

Q: How can I keep my dog from getting diarrhea if I switch his dog food?
A: Try adding some boiled potatoes in with his new food. Rice works too but is more fattening.

Our Own Rescues – Some Observations

If you already have pets, one of the more interesting things about bringing in a new dog or cat is seeing how your pets react to the newcomer. We have always tried to be cautious and keep a close eye on things, especially if the newcomer is a puppy or kitten. You just can't always predict how things are going to go though.

For example we already had Jade (a 4-year old three-legged female Rottweiler) when we brought in Harley Cole, a six-week old Labradane pup. We were more than a little nervous about Jade's reaction to Cole; given her size and strength we wanted to make sure Jade wouldn't suddenly decide to simply dispose of the pup.

Instead of being aggressive though, Jade was just the opposite. She holed up in our bedroom, looked depressed and only rarely came out into the living room when we had Cole out. All we could figure out was that Jade (who had been dumped at a shelter twice before) must have decided that the pup had been brought in to replace her and that we were about to get rid of her. It took several weeks before she began to act normally again.

Once Jade began to hang out with us Cole would run over to her and try to play-fight. For about a week we hovered around close to them since Jade could have killed him in an instant - and because her "play-fighting" consisted largely of snarling, bowling the pup over, and putting her jaws around his throat.

Finally though it dawned on us that Jade actually LIKED the pup and was simply trying to teach him how to be a proper Rottweiler. For the rest of the time Jade was with us the relationship between her and Harley Cole was very much like a proud mother and her son.

On the other hand we brought in a kitten several years ago that my daughter Cathey had adopted from the city pound. The kitten had a minor health problem that required a visit to the vet and some medication but other than that she was a cute, playful, happy creature.

The kitten, now fully grown, has been with us for about five years and shows no signs of bad temper or bad behavior of any kind. However none of our other cats can stand her – it doesn't often break out into full-scale warfare but there is obviously no love lost between her and the rest of our felines. I would give a great deal to know what it is about her that gets other cats so hostile but Sassy is a perfect example of the fact that sometimes you just can't predict how existing pets will react to a newcomer.

Considering the ridiculously large number of rescue animals we have brought into the house over the years and the fact that Sassy is the only instance where we've had a problem, I'm willing to bet that bringing rescue pets into a household that already has pets usually works out just fine.

However, if you are planning on adopting a dog or cat from a shelter and the shelter offers a "familiarization" area where you can bring your children and pets to meet the potential newcomer, you should take advantage of that opportunity. No matter how attracted you are to a certain dog or cat and no matter how convinced you are that he or she will be a perfect fit for your family, take a little time for a "test drive" just to make sure.

Our Own Rescues - Jade

For most of my life I knew virtually nothing about Rottweilers; or more accurately I knew a number of things that weren't true. For example, I pictured Rottweilers as very aggressive guard dogs that didn't make good pets and weren't "people" dogs. Then about five years ago while browsing the internet looking at dogs up for adoption, my daughter fell in love with "Jade", a two-year old three-legged female Rottie at a shelter in Texas. A few weeks later we were on our way to Texas to adopt Jade -- a move which led to a quick re-education on my part as to the truth about Rottweilers.

When we first met Jade my impression was of a large, lurching bear of a dog, tongue hanging out one side of her mouth and stub tail wagging furiously. She had lost her right front leg when she was hit by a car as a puppy. Her owners paid to have her leg amputated but decided they no longer wanted her and dropped her off at the local animal shelter. Then an older couple adopted her to replace their dog who had died, but quickly decided Jade wasn't the right dog for them. They ended up dropping her at another shelter which is where we eventually found her.

Once we got back home with the newest member of our family a couple of things quickly became apparent. Rottweiler experts will tell you that you need to establish control over your Rottie early on or it will become very hard to manage. In Jade's case establishing control was a real challenge. After spending half her life in a kennel she had obviously decided that humans, although nice enough, weren't to be trusted. It wasn't that she was uncontrollable -- it was more a case of Jade having developed a strong sense of independence. Getting her to do what you wanted took a certain amount of give and take.

I did learn several things about Rotties while we were working on getting more control over Jade. First of all, I did some reading and found out that Rottweilers were actually bred as herding dogs and were also used to pull small loads; only later on were they used as guard dogs. They are in fact "people" dogs and enjoy spending a lot of time with their humans. Rotties are strong, tough, loyal -- and as subtle as a sledgehammer. By nature they tend to be loud (Jade has a snarl that could peel paint off a wall), suspicious of strangers (outside of the house at least), and patient (their ability to remain calm and not over-react to situations is one quality that makes them good guard dogs).

As mentioned, Rotties usually like to "hang out" with their humans, but it took several months for Jade to really warm up to us. She would spend most of her time alone in the bedroom and rarely got up and moved around except to go outside. She got so little exercise that she began to put on weight and, since it took a certain amount of effort for her to get up with only three legs, she even started to drag herself around at times rather than go to the trouble of heaving herself up on her feet. Eventually an improved diet of weight maintenance dog chow and green beans took most of the weight back off and Cole, a Lab pup we rescued, gave Jade someone to play with and got her back up and moving around.

Now, five years later, Jade is an integral part of our family and I've learned several more truths about Rotties:

- Experts say you need to brush your Rottweiler at least once a week to comb out the loose fur from their undercoat and that's the absolute truth. Brushing Jade is a major operation -- my wife (who Jade has adopted as her human) usually spends 30 minutes or more brushing her and even uses an attachment on the vacuum cleaner to try to suck up all the loose fur (and by the way, Jade seems to enjoy being vacuumed).

Rotties are also supposed to be sensitive to both hot and cold weather. Considering the thickness of her undercoat, Jade does have a problem with really hot weather. We only let her out for a short time during the day in the summer. As for not tolerating really cold weather, I'm not sure I entirely agree with that. I've seen Jade lie outside in the snow for several hours at a time and have to be coaxed back into the house.

- Another "truth" I've discovered about Rotties that you don't read much about is the "gas" problem. Everyone we've talked to who has a Rottweiler seems to share this problem. You'll be sitting there and suddenly your Rottie expels some gas. Within moments the room becomes enveloped in a haze of noxious gas. This room-clearing effect probably has something to do with improper diet, but none of the owners we know have found an answer for it yet.

Experts also caution you not to give your Rottie rawhide. Jade does get rawhide chips, but not large pieces. Besides which, Cole (our Lab) generally steals them from her before Jade has a chance to consume much of the rawhide. Oddly enough though, Jade does have a passion for paper products; leave a Kleenex, paper towel or napkin within her reach and she'll down it in one gulp.

One thing I've found to be especially true is that you do need to be careful about strangers and other animals. Inside our house Jade is always happy to greet new people and even at the pet store she's friendly enough to others. Outside our house though Jade becomes much more cautious and can be very aggressive toward strangers at times (although since Rotties consider a bull rush and chest bump as a proper greeting, sometimes it's hard to tell hostility from enthusiasm). As for other animals, Jade gets along fine with our Lab, our cats and our parrots, but you can never be quite sure how she's going to react to a new animal.

Finally, Rottweilers are surprisingly intelligent (the ninth-most intelligent dog breed according to a recent study). With their size, strength, and somewhat aggressive nature it's easy to assume that they're not too bright. Be aware though, inside that titanium steel skull is an active, problem-solving mind.

All in all, we've become very attached to our brute of a dog. Jade may drool, pass gas, shed and let out ear-splitting snarls, but she's also a lovable, sometimes clownish, sometimes sensitive, and always entertaining member of our family.

NOTE: We lost Jade to lung cancer in June 2011 – we miss our three-legged bear of a dog.

Our Own Rescues - Harley Cole

Harley Cole is our Lab. Well, actually he appears to have some Great Dane mixed in, so technically he's a "Labradane" - all 105 pounds of him.

Cole was part of a litter of pups belonging to a single mother who lived next door to my mother. The woman bred her Lab so she could have some pups to sell but while she was trying to find buyers the pups were stuck in the back yard and only rarely got any food or water. Mom tried to make sure they at least had some water and an occasional bowl of dog chow but the pups were barely getting by. And then the mother and her kids moved out, leaving three male puppies there in her back yard.

At that point we went and collected the pups and brought them to our house so we could try to find homes for them. We placed two of them without any problem but no one really wanted the black pup. As days went by we finally decided to keep him – a fateful decision as it turned out.

That pup - Harley Cole - was born on April 1st , which should have been a warning sign. A little over two weeks after we took him in he managed to set fire to our house. As near as we can figure out, he got up and went into the kitchen about 2 o'clock on a Sunday morning and while trying to get to a pizza box lying next to the stove, he somehow managed to push the box over onto a burner and turn the ignitor switch on the burner.

The smoke alarm going off woke up my wife but by that time the pizza box had caught fire and that set one of the cabinets on fire. My daughter Cathey and I tried to put out the blaze with a fire extinguisher, but only managed to douse part of it. After calling 911 Sandy, Cathey and I wound up frantically shoving birds into makeshift carrying cages and trying to get the birds, cats and dogs outside.

When the whole mess was over we ended up with about fifteen thousand dollars worth of damage to the house – which makes Cole the most expensive animal we've ever rescued. "Pyro Pup" came close to being banished from the premises forever, but in the end we decided it was mostly our fault for leaving the pizza box in the wrong place and just a freak accident that Cole had been able to turn the burner on somehow while pawing at the box.

In any case that was five years ago now and the little pup who slept on our bed the first couple of weeks to help him feel more secure now plants his hundred pounds plus on the bed each night and serves as my alarm clock. Cole faithfully wakes me up at 4:30 or so every morning (seven days a week) to let me know he's hungry and it's time for chow.

Raising Cole has been interesting and I've learned a few things about Labrador Retrievers (or Labradanes) in the process. For one thing, Labs take somewhat longer to grow out of the puppy stage than most breeds. In the case of a male, you can figure on it taking about 3 years for him to reach adulthood.

I've also discovered that Labs tend to be very intelligent. If you've ever read those stories about a Lab getting in his or her owner's car and managing to put it in gear - or pawing at a computer mouse while the computer was online and ending up putting several hundred dollars on the owner's credit card – well, those are in fact the kind of things Labs do. They require close supervision at all times – at least until they hit that 3 year old mark.

Labs are also very inquisitive by nature. If you have a plumber or other repairman come into the house, be prepared for your Lab to try to help with whatever the repair job is. Labs are always looking to learn new skills. And if you take your Lab for a ride in your car, it's definitely a good idea to make him or her sit in back – I've learned from personal experience that Harley Cole is anxious to learn how to drive and is perfectly willing to get in my lap and take the wheel.

I've also learned that Labs tend to be sneaky by nature. Cole is well-behaved in the house for the most part, but he does have one failing. From time to time he likes to go back in the utility room and see what he can find in the trash can that looks appealing. If he finds something he will lift it out carefully, look around to see if anyone's watching, and then duck his head and walk rapidly through the living room and into the bedroom as nonchalantly as possible. If one of us spots him and calls out to him, Cole will drop whatever he has and look around as if he has no idea where it came from.

One last thing I've learned about Labs is that they have very big mouths. Cole likes to keep track of his "stuff" and you will often see him walking around with 2 or 3 toys and a rawhide chew in his mouth. On a couple of occasions he has even brought his large, heavy ceramic water dish in to me to let me know that it needs refilling.

Cole is also very possessive. When Bill and Melinda (my daughter and son-in-law) came to visit and brought their dog, Cole quickly gathered up all his favorite toys, carried them upstairs and hid them in one of the bedrooms. Outside of that he was a good host to their dog "Boomer", but he definitely got a "doesn't share well with others" on his report card for that visit.

Sometimes when Cole is asking to go out front for the fifth time in 20 minutes (to look for the squirrel who lives in our oak tree) the thought crosses my mind that we should have tried harder to find him a home. The truth is though that I would find it hard to get to sleep at night if I didn't have him crammed up against me. And then too, how would I wake up in the morning without my furry alarm clock?

Our Own Rescues – Ashley

We found Ashley wandering around outside my wife's parents house one day and after a number of attempts to find his owners we finally decided to keep him. Ash was a male mixed breed who was mostly Russian Blue. He was also smart (you might even say devious) and very active.

My favorite memory of Ash involved a steak my wife and I had splurged on and bought for a Saturday night dinner. Sandy, my wife, had the steak lying out on the kitchen counter, ready to cook, while she got a few other things out of the refrigerator. When she called me in to start the grill the steak was nowhere to be found – until we looked down the hallway toward the bedrooms. There was Ash, determinedly pulling the steak along, trying to get it into one of the bedrooms before we noticed him. Considering how much of our weekly budget the steak had consumed, we washed it off thoroughly and cooked it anyway.

Ash also was a great hunter. He loved to have me hold him up while he tried to swat flies or moths out of the air or trap one between his paws. He was darned good at it too and we made a great team.

When our first daughter came along we decided we needed to keep a close eye on Ash. As active as he was we didn't want him jumping into her crib and landing on top of her. We shouldn't have worried. Ashley "adopted" Melinda and would lie in the doorway to her bedroom at night and keep watch. If she woke up and began to fuss, Ash would come find us and let us know that Melinda was awake and we needed to go take care of her. For a male cat Ash made a great nanny.

Our Own Rescues - Rambo

We came home one afternoon over twenty years ago and found a large male cat lying against our front door. We moved him out of the way and went inside figuring he would move on shortly. The next day when my wife got home there he was again, lying against the front door. This went on for about two weeks until one day our large feline friend simply slipped inside when we opened the front door. After a few attempts to evict him we finally gave up and added him to our menagerie.

That turned out to be one of the best moves we ever made. The large cat was a Maine Coon, a breed once described as "humans in a cat suit". Rambo (short for a long string of names my daughters bestowed upon him) was, according to our vet, about 8 years old when he adopted us. We finally had to put him to sleep some 20 years later and it was very much like losing a human member of the family.

Things didn't exactly start off that way however. My older daughter Melinda was a gymnast and had a fairly expensive practice balance beam in the living room. The second day Rambo was in the house he decided to climb around on the beam and use it as a scratching post. I ran back and forth trying to shoo him off the beam and he kept pulling himself along the bottom of the beam raking it with his claws as he went. I finally chased him off, but it was obvious he didn't understand what I was so worked up about.

Regardless, things settled down for a while after that – until he decided to show his gratitude to us by bringing in his share of the food. He tried twice to deposit a nice, tasty mouse in the front hallway and ended up with Sandy's mother Nancy chasing him out of the house with a broom each time. Eventually he got the idea that we would supply all the chow inside and he could keep his snacks outside.

For an older tomcat Rambo was amazingly well-behaved when he was in the house (although he hunted and defended his turf outside with a passion). We had a hamster amble slowly past him and one of our parrots land right in front of him and Rambo never batted an eye. Even more impressive, he would fight any cat that wandered into our yard, but simply moved out of the way when one of the inside cats tried to pick a fight with him.

Rambo also had a slightly twisted sense of humor. We had a large tree next to our driveway and every once in a while on dark winter mornings Rambo would drop out of the tree onto the roof of my car with a loud thump just as I got in – a great way to start your day and get your heart beating. And once he got to the point where he completely trusted us, he also found it amusing to saunter out into the driveway and flop down just as we pulled in – forcing us to stop, get out, pick him up and move him out of the way.

Christmas was really Rambo's favorite time of the year and he thoroughly enjoyed the Christmas lights we strung outside. He would follow us around everywhere as we put the lights up – and I mean everywhere. On one occasion I climbed up a ladder to string lights along the roof only to turn around and see Rambo perched on the top rung of the ladder watching me with great interest. Believe me, it's not easy backing down a ladder carrying a 20 pound cat.

It was also a treat watching Rambo outside in the snow. Maine Coon cats - the official state cat of Maine by the way- have oversize paws that act like snowshoes. While our dogs were sinking into the snow, Rambo glided over it as if he was walking on water (which he was come to think of it).

Now Rambo's urn sits on our fireplace mantle in a place of honor, along with his picture. Of all the cats we've adopted over the years, he will always be the one that we were lucky enough to have adopt us.

Our Own Rescues - Gabriel

About five years ago we acquired another rescue bird, a female umbrella cockatoo named Gabriel. Not Gabrielle – Gabriel (as she will quickly point out if you mispronounce her name). She had been found outside someone's home after she "flew" into their yard (quite a feat since there were so few feathers on her wings that she wasn't capable of flying).

At first we thought she was very young because she was small for an umbrella cockatoo and had very few feathers on her breast. After checking the breeder's tag though we realized that Gaby was thirteen – still fairly young for a cockatoo since they can live to be 70 or more, but considerably older than we had thought. She was simply stunted and had plucked out most of her feathers – a sure sign of a bird that is in bad shape emotionally.

The details aren't important but we also quickly figured out that Gabriel had been pretty badly abused. She immediately attached herself to my younger daughter Cathey, but men (myself included) terrified her. If I came near her with a magazine or newspaper in my hand she would either scream and jump off her cage or huddle in a back corner of the cage, muttering to herself "I love Gabriel", "I love Gabriel."

It also became clear that she didn't have any idea of how to play with bird toys and was extremely nervous about someone moving quickly in her direction. In fact a lot of different things terrified her and would start her screaming.

In our case Gabriel was so traumatized that she didn't make much of a ruckus at first. Slowly, over a period of a year or two she began to adjust to her new home. We moved her into a larger cage, made sure she got plenty of food (and the right kind of food) and we introduced her to a variety of bird toys. She eventually stopped plucking her feathers and quit being scared of so many things.

Now she spends most of her day outside of her cage, climbing around, playing with her toys and watching everything going on around her. She has even invented a couple of games that she likes to play with me (when she's not trying to bite me). Her favorite game is "Where's Gaby?" where she hides under the cover on top of her cage and I'm supposed to try to find her – without looking at where she's actually hiding of course.

Gabriel is also still very attached to my daughter Cathey. When Cathey puts Gabriel somewhere next to her, Gaby usually spends most of her time marching back and forth with her crest up, watching in all directions and guarding her "Mommy".

Gabriel's rehabilitation has even reached the point where she's looking to open communications with our cats. The other day she jumped off her cage, bunny-hopped over to our cat RJ, stopped right in front of him and said "hello?", "hello?". RJ stared for a moment and then bolted for the bedroom, obviously not ready for a meaningful conversation with a cockatoo.

Gaby is always going to be somewhat like an autistic child (for example she hates any change in the daily routine) but she's a much happier cockatoo these days, with many years ahead of her. I'm still convinced that cockatoos probably shouldn't be sold as pets, but at least this cockatoo is on the road to recovery.

Note: Cockatoos can be very noisy (ear-splitting at times) especially if no one pays any attention to them. Unfortunately many people get baby cockatoos because they are cute, cuddly and very affectionate. New owners tend to spend a good deal of time handling the young bird and the cockatoo forms a strong bond with its human(s). Later when the newness wears off the owner or owners don't want to spend as much time with the bird – but the cockatoo doesn't understand that and starts to scream for attention. Just something to be aware of if you ever decide to pick a cockatoo as a pet.

Our Own Rescues - Kitty

Kitty was pretty much just your average cat (with a very average name) and I mention her just because of how she came to live with us. It was the dead of winter with snow and ice on the ground and my wife Sandy and I had just agreed that there would be no more rescue animals. We had a number of them running around the house and it was a major drain on our meager budget back then just to keep up with the bills for food, litter, toys, vet checkups, etc.

We had driven to a convenience store near the house to pick up a few things, fighting our way through the snow. I went inside to buy whatever it was we needed and when I came back out there was a small kitten on our car – wrapped around the aerial, mewing and hanging on for dear life.

I looked at Sandy, she looked at me and we both stared at the kitten who was mewing even louder. At that point about all we could do was laugh, pry "Kitty" off the aerial and take her home with us. Sometimes I think we're doomed to keep finding strays like this – no matter how many times we decide that we've done our share, another homeless cat, dog, bird or other creature always seems to come along.

Other Stuff – Acupuncture

A friend of ours who works at a local veterinary office stopped by the other day and happened to mention that she had a set of acupuncture needles and was learning how to use them. When I asked who she was going to use them on, she said that the veterinarian at her clinic intended to start offering acupuncture as an option for some of the pets that came in for treatment. Later I did a little research on the internet and it appears that her clinic isn't alone -- a good many veterinarians are turning to alternative medicine in certain cases, particularly the use of acupuncture.

According to traditional Eastern medicine, acupuncture is considered to be a method of correcting an imbalance in the flow of energy (or "qi") along certain pathways or "meridians" in the body. Small needles inserted in any of hundreds of specified acupuncture "points" redirect the flow of energy and restore the body to health. Western medicine explains the effectiveness of acupuncture by pointing out that most of these acupuncture points are located at clusters of nerves and blood vessels. Stimulating those areas through the insertion of small needles can trigger a number of reactions including increased blood flow, the release of endorphins (the body's pain regulators), and the release of smaller amounts of cortisol, the body's own anti-inflammatory drug. The improved biochemical balance that acupuncture produces stimulates the body's natural healing abilities and promotes physical and emotional well-being.

Today veterinarians are using acupuncture to treat various conditions including chronic pain, digestive disorders, hip dysplasia, allergies, asthma, neurological problems and urinary tract disorders. Even behavioral issues can sometimes by alleviated through acupuncture treatments. Of course acupuncture by itself doesn't cure disease but it can help the body to heal itself by altering various physiological and biochemical factors.

An acupuncture session will usually involve inserting very thin needles (about the diameter of a thick hair) along the animal's bladder, kidney, and spleen meridians. The animal is conscious during the entire process and shouldn't experience any discomfort; in fact most animals actually tend to become relaxed during a typical session. The size and exact location of the needles varies depending on the size of the animal and the type of illness being treated, with short needles about half an inch in length being used on areas around the head while longer one-inch needles are used elsewhere. A typical session may last anywhere from a couple of minutes to a half hour, although a particularly complicated case can take somewhat longer. If the treatment is done by someone who is trained and experienced, acupuncture is a very safe procedure and you should see some improvement in the animal's condition in a few days or a few weeks at most.

There are numerous documented examples of the successful use of animal acupuncture. In one instance, a woman's 16 year old border collie was diagnosed with kidney disease. Traditional veterinary medicine gave the owner two options -- dialysis or euthanasia. The collie's owner chose another option - acupuncture - and for over a year now acupuncture treatments have helped alleviate the border collie's symptoms and have relieved much of the discomfort. The disease hasn't been cured, but acupuncture has prolonged the dog's life and has done it in a way that provides a decent quality of life.

Another example from a local veterinary clinic involves a 12 year old German Shepard with degenerative spinal disease. The shepherd gets weekly treatments using a number of needles in his back to maintain feeling in his spine and other needles at points in his lower legs to preserve feeling in his toes. There isn't any surgical cure for his condition and without these treatments he would soon begin to lose the use of his back legs.

While the examples above both involved dogs, acupuncture can be applied to dogs, cats, ferrets, rabbits, horses, cows, and even birds. Veterinarians first began to use acupuncture in the 1970's and today it's rapidly becoming an accepted part of the veterinarian's arsenal as an alternative to or in addition to drugs and surgery. It may or may not be something you would choose to have used on your pet -- but it's certainly something to think about when you look at the growing number of successes in providing help for animals, particularly those who have run out of traditional treatment options.

NOTE: Chiropractic care is also being integrated into veterinary practice to some extent as a possible treatment for chronic back and neck pain or disk disease.

Other Stuff – Animal Signing

Have you ever wanted to sit down and have a conversation with your dog? Or just ask your pooch "Why are you barking?" Well, that just might be possible according to Sean Senechal. In her book "Dogs Can Sign, Too", she presents a method for communicating with your canine -- a system of gestures that she calls "K9Signs" which could allow your dog to "talk" to you. The goal is to teach dogs to use this sign language to ask for things, to ask or answer questions, and to respond to your commands or comments.

Senechal has established an "academy" (the AnimalSign Center) where people are working every day with dogs and other animals to see just what their limits are as "language learners". The author emphasizes that it will probably be years before any definite conclusions can be drawn as to the ability of non-primate animals to communicate with us, but she offers a number of examples of what she has accomplished in working with her own pets.

One example had to do with her dog Chal who she has worked with for several years. Chal came into a room where Senechal was talking to a friend and tapped a storage drawer with her nose, then lifted her right front leg which is the K9Sign for an object. When Senechal made the sign for "What?", Chal lifted her right front leg and flicked it slightly, the sign for "keys". The author opened the drawer and there was the key to the yard gate; Chal immediately ran out to the gate and waited for Senechal to open it for her.

That story may not seem all that unusual or interesting; after all I had a border collie whose parents herded cattle and sheep and were able to respond to a wide variety of hand and voice signals. The main difference is that in Chal's case she not only responds to various signs, she offers her own canine signs. If you thought Lassie was brilliant, imagine a herd dog that could come to you and sign "Lamb caught under branch in gully over there; wildcat sneaking up on her -- hurry". That's the fascinating part of K9Signs; not just the ability to communicate but the complexity of the information that can be exchanged in just a few signs.

K9Signs training, as Senechal points out, is fundamentally different from obedience training. It calls for encouraging your dog to show creative behavior rather than obedience. Your dog has to be prompted to initiate communication and make requests rather than just respond to commands. Conversation implies a give and take, a two-sided method of communicating and that means your dog has to feel free to "talk back".

Maybe the most important thing to remember in K9Sign training is to make signing fun. If your dog is obviously having trouble understanding what you're doing and seems to be getting frustrated or losing interest, back up and try to break the lesson down into simpler steps and reward the accomplishment of each smaller step. Or go back to something your dog has already learned and enjoys (like playing with a favorite toy) and make that sign. Later you can go back to working on the new sign. Senechal constantly emphasizes the importance of patience, rewards, and slow, easy steps in teaching K9Signs.

I'm not sure I would have the patience for K9Sign training and really, like most dogs, my two already communicate with me without animal signing. For example my Lab will bark and let me know if someone comes to the front door. But if he and I could make use of K9Signs, who knows -- maybe he could tell me "Pat at front door, has pizza" or "Two strange men at front door, smell friendly". Or instead of simply moving around restlessly, maybe our Rottweiler could tell me "Feel bad - need go out and eat grass". It would require a good deal of time and patience, but maybe one of these days I'll work up the courage to give K9Signs a try (and find out what my dogs are really thinking).

If you're interested in learning more about Sean Senechal's K9Signs system or her method of animal signing in general, her books "AnimalSigns To You" and "Dogs Can Sign Too", are both available for sale online.

Appendix A – Adopting a Parrot

1) Before you bring home a new parrot make sure you have a cage that's large enough and that has bars that are close enough together that the bird can't squeeze through them.
2) Wash the cage once you get it home and assembled - parrots aren't as delicate as some sources would have you believe, but they do tend to rub their beaks on the cage so you want to make sure the cage is clean.
3) Buy a decent brand of the appropriate size of bird food for your parrot (ask at your local pet store or check online if you're not sure what type and size to buy).
4) Most parrots will eat the seeds or other items in their food dish and leave the bulk of the empty hulls or other debris in the dish. Empty and refill your bird's food dish every day or two - it may look as if it's still almost full, but you're probably looking at a bunch of inedible leftovers.
5) Check the water dish every day. Parrots not only drink from their water dish, they may also try to take a bath in it - or just splash water out for the heck of it.
6) Line the bottom of the cage with newspaper to catch the spilled seeds, bird poop, or anything else that hits the bottom of the cage and change the papers every week or so. Note: you should also try to wipe down any other parts of the cage that get dirty - most birds are

a little on the messy side and are notoriously poor housekeepers.

7) Make sure you have at least a couple of perches in the cage. Parrots spend most of their time standing (and sleeping) on a perch and they need one that's the right size for their claws and preferably one that's somewhat rough so that it keeps their claws from growing too long. Oh, and parrots generally like their perches to be higher up in the cage (but low enough that there head isn't right up against the top of the cage).

8) Different species of parrots have different IQs (most smaller parrots for instance have approximately the IQ of a 3 year old human), but they all appreciate having something to do besides sit on a perch all day. Buy a few bird toys and change them every so often - your bird will thank you.

9) Give your bird a shower occasionally. Fill a spray bottle with some lukewarm water and spray your bird gently. Note: there may be some days when they're not in the mood for a shower - if so, try again in a day or so.

10) Keep some cornstarch or styptic powder handy - if your parrot breaks a blood feather it may bleed freely and can cause considerable blood loss in a hurry. The cornstarch or styptic powder will help stop the blood flow.

11) Be aware – chlamydiosis (psittacosis) and avian tuberculosis can be transmitted through the air from birds to humans. Also, parrots continually shed "feather dust" which can aggravate asthma in some people. A HEPA-

type filter in rooms with parrots can help control problems from bird dander.

12) Most parrots have long life spans – as long as 70 years. Adopting a parrot can be a life-long experience.

13) Parrots are sensitive to air quality. Unlike humans they completely exhaust the air in their lungs with each breath and consequently they take in more oxygen and pollutants with each breath. Parrots shouldn't be exposed to tobacco smoke, fumes from hair spray or air fresheners, or fumes from Teflon coated cooking utensils.

Author's note: While it's certainly true that parrots can become sick or die from breathing in fumes of one type or another, they may not be as delicate as some articles would have you believe. Several years ago our six parrots survived a house fire and a significant amount of smoke while we were getting them into carriers and out of the house. All six survived and are perfectly healthy.

Appendix B – Useful Pet Web Sites

- http://animal.discovery.com/petsource/ - includes information on cats, dogs, birds, fish, horses and reptiles, as well as pet videos, videos on caring for your pets and games to play.
- http://petfinder.com – research cats and dogs by breed, look at animals up for adoption at shelters all around the country, and find advice about adopting and caring for a shelter pet.
- http://www.aspca.org/pet-care/ - detailed guides on nutrition, behavior, emergency care and pet care in general.
- http://www.humanesociety.org – home of the largest animal protection organization in the United States. The Humane Society also publishes two bimonthly magazines - "All Animals" for members and "Animal Sheltering" for shelter workers.
- http://www.bestfriends.org – largest animal sanctuary in the U.S. and they publish "Best Friends" magazine.
- http://www.petco.com/CareSheets/petco_Care Sheets_Nav_154.aspx – PETCO animal care sheets.
- http://vetblog.co.uk/vetblog/ - Vet Blog, a web magazine for pet owners.
- http://www.facebook.com/group.php? gid=113118818720431 – Exotic animal rescue society.
- http://www.birdsupplies.com/Trick-Training-Bird-Toys-s/42.htm – Educational bird toys.

Appendix C – Additional Resources

- **"One at a Time: A Week in an American Animal Shelter"** by Diane Leigh and Marilee Gever. Chronicles the true stories of 75 animals who entered a typical U.S. animal shelter during one week as witnessed and documented by the authors.
- **"Rescue Matters: How to Find, Foster, and Rehome Companion Animals: A Guide for Volunteers and Organizers"** by Sheila Webster Boneham. Covers the legal, organizational, and paperwork needs of rescue groups as well as finding and working with volunteers. Also deals with the animals themselves; how to evaluate (health issues, personality assessment, type of home needed) foster homes and veterinary card, assessing potential adopters, training, and dealing with behavioral problems.
- **"The First Aid Companion for Dogs & Cats"** by Amy D. Shojai. Covers basic first aid techniques, what to keep in your pet's medicine chest, how to quickly determine what's wrong with your pet, plus a detailed guide to over 150 injuries and conditions and what to do about each one.

Appendix D – Dog Height/Weight Chart

Breed	Height (inches)	Weight (pounds)
Airdale Terrier	22-24	44-50
Akita	23-28	65-130
American Bulldog	19-28	65-130
American Eskimo (Std)	15-19	20-40
Australian Shepherd	18-23	35-70
Basset Hound	12-14	40-60
Beagle	13-15	18-30
Bichon Frise	9.5-11.5	7-12
Bloodhound	23-37	80-110
Border Collie	18-23	30-45
Boston Terrier	15-17	10-25
Boxer	21-25	45-80
Bull Mastiff	24-27	110-130
Bull Terrier	21-22	45-65
Cairn Terrier	9.5-10	13-14
Cavalier King Charles Spaniel	12-13	13-18
Chesapeake Bay Retriever	21-26	55-80
Chihuahua	6-9	2-6
Chinese Crested	11-13	5-12
Chinese Shar-pei	18-20	45-60
Chow Chow	17-20	40-70
Cocker Spaniel	13.5-15.5	24-28
Collie	22-26	50-75
Dachshund (Std)	8-9	16-32
Dachshund (Miniature)	5-10	9-10
Dalmation	19-23	40-65
Doberman Pinscher	24-28	65-90
English Bulldog	12-15	40-50
English Mastiff	27-30	170-190
Fox Terrier	14-15.5	16-18
German Shepherd	22-26	75-95
Golden Retriever	21.5-24	55-75
Great Dane	28-32	100-120
Italian Greyhound	10-12	12-15

Jack Russell Terrier	12-15	13-17
Labrador Retriever	21-24.5	55-80
Lhasa Apso	9-11	13-15
Maltese	9-10	4-7
Miniature Pinscher	10-12.5	8-10
Old English Sheepdog	21-24	65-70
Papillon	8-11	9-10
Pekinese	6-9	6-14
Pembroke Welsh Corgi	10-12	25-37
Pomeranian	8-11	3-7
Poodle (Miniature)	11-15	26-30
Poodle (Standard)	15-22	45-70
Poodle (Toy)	8-10	14-16.5
Pug	10-11	14-18
Rat Terrier	8-14	6-8
Rottweiler	22-27	70-125
Saint Bernard	25-27.5	120-200
Samoyed	19-23.5	30-65
Schipperke	10-13	12-16
Shetland Sheepdog	13-16	15-20
Weimaraner	23-27	70-85
West Highland Terrier	10-11	15-21
Yorkshire Terrier	8-9	4-7

Appendix E – Sample Adoption Form

Note: An example of a shelter adoption questionnaire is shown below to give you an idea of what this type of form is like. Some people looking to adopt a pet from a shelter are surprised or upset when they are handed one of these. Keep in mind that the purpose is to help the shelter to help you to find the right pet – and to try to make sure you understand the responsibility involved in adopting and that you're willing and able to assume that responsibility.

Sample Adoption Questionnaire

Name: _____
Address: _____ City: _____
State: _____ Zip:_____ Phone: _____

Length of time at this address: _____
Own ___ Rent ___ Live with parents ___
Housing type:
    Home ____ Apartment ____ Mobile Home ____

How did you hear about our shelter: _____

Current veterinarian: _____

Employer/Phone No. _____
Drivers license#/State/Expiration: _____
Date of Birth: _____
Number of children living with you & ages: _____

How long have you lived at your current address: __

_____

Are you planning to move in the next 6 months? _____

Have you ever had to move? _____
Did you take your pets with you? _____
If you have to move in the future do you plan to take
your pets with you? _____
Who will be responsible for your pets care? _____

Is there anyone in your household who doesn't want
a pet? _____
Is anyone in your household allergic to animals? _____

Have you ever owned a pet before? _____
If yes, what happened to it?
_____
How long did you have it? _____
Was it spayed or neutered? _____

What pets do you currently own? (Please list all
including breed, name and whether they are spayed
or neutered)
Pet#1 _____
Pet#2 _____
Pet#3 _____
Pet#4 _____
Pet#5 _____
Pet#6 _____

Have you ever had to take a pet to a shelter or pound? _____
If yes, why? _____

What is your main reason for wanting a pet?
    Companion _____
    Watch dog _____
    Mouser _____
    For the children _____
    Friend for other pets _____
    Other _____

What type of pet do you want:
    Active _____   Affectionate _____   Playful _____
    Quiet _____   Gentle _____   Protective ____

Do you need your new pet to get along with:
    Dogs ____   Cats ____   Children _____

Do you believe in spaying and neutering? ____
Why or why not? _____

Where will your pet spend most of it's time?

_____

Will this pet be allowed in the house? _____
How long will it be left alone each day? _____
Where will it sleep at night? _____
If outside what kind of shelter is available?

_____

Do you plan to ID your new pet? _____

If you had to give up this pet what would you do?

_____

_____

Signature: _____ Date: _____

Alphabetical Index

Notes

Notes

2739401R00070

Made in the USA
San Bernardino, CA
30 May 2013